F*ck Toxic Spirituality

F*ck Toxic Spirituality

Avoiding Red Flags & Navigating the Spiritual Path with Integrity

Katie Turner, M.Sc, R.Psych.

Katie Turner Psychology Inc.

This book contains information that is intended to help readers to be better informed consumers of health care and mental health care. It is not intended as a substitute for professional medical advice, assessment, diagnosis or treatment. There are many sources of different symptoms and I am offering one perspective. Though I am a Registered Psychologist, I am not your Psychologist, (unless we have a pre-existing professional therapeutic relationship). Reading this book does not create a therapeutic relationship between us. This book should not be used as a substitute for the advice of a competent mental health professional authorized to practice in your jurisdiction. Be sure to use your own wise judgment and consult your own doctor and/or mental health professional for your individual needs.

The information provided within this book is for general informational purposes only. While every effort has been made to keep the information up-to-date and correct, there are no representations or warranties, express or implied, about the completeness, accuracy, reliability, sustainability or availability with respect to the information, products, services or related graphics contained in this book for any purpose.

The author and publisher of this book is not responsible for any specific health or lethal health needs that may require medical supervision and is not liable for any damages or negative consequences from any treatment, action, application or preparation, to any person reading or following the information in this book. References are provided for informational purposes only and do not constitute endorsement of any websites or other sources. Readers should be aware that the websites listed in this book may change.

Use the information in this book at your own risk.

For permission requests, write to the author at:

info@katieturner.ca

Katie Turner

Katie Turner Psychology Inc.

www.katieturnerpsychology.com

F*ck Toxic Spirituality: Avoiding Red Flags & Navigating the
Spiritual Path with Integrity / Katie Turner—1st ed.

ISBN 978-1-7382852-0-4

First of all, I wish to express a heartfelt thank you to my clients, past and present. It has been an honour and privilege to be a part of your journey. Without you, this work would not be possible.

On a larger scale, I dedicate this book to all those who have made the commitment to their own healing path. To the cycle breakers and change agents. To all those who aspire to be a better version of themselves. To those who are leading with love and who dare to dream of a better future for everyone.

For all those who feel the calling within their own soul, for the connection with something greater - the source from which we all come from and to which we will return. You may call it source, universe, god/goddess, the infinite, or any term that makes the most sense to you.

May this calling continue to inspire your search for your own connection with this part of your soul. May it help guide you to your own personal resonance with something much greater.

May this guidebook help to bring you back to yourself and remind you why you are on this path. You are an integral part of the strong, quiet force that is transforming this world. May we all hold the vision of a more loving and safe reality for everyone.

Even the smallest movements of positive change create ripple effects... Often beyond our wildest dreams.

You matter.

Your healing journey matters.

Together, we are helping to co-create a better world.

With deepest love and gratitude,

Katie Turner

As a self-declared spiritual seeker and psychiatrist for 30 years, I was rewarded to read Katie's book on toxic spirituality, both for the wisdom that is required to illuminate the spiritual path and the tenderness with which she approaches the subject.

Having worked with and witnessed Katie's skills for many years in different settings, as a student, teacher, and mentor, she continues to bring a warm conversational style when addressing the benefits of feeling more grounded in a disorienting world where exhaustion, stress, and mental health are common concerns. While progress has been in making well-being a focus of our lives, and despite easy access to mental health support in the digital space, the mental health crisis continues to grow.

There is growing awareness that spiritual health is essential for mental health and Katie offers a vision of how spirituality could make a significant contribution toward greater well-being and flourishing. While the spiritual path can be seductive, and at times blissfully calm, it requires patience, humility, wise counsel, guidance and trustworthy mentorship to benefit from its healing powers. Katie brings an honest blend of personal and professional reflections in exploring the world of the human spirit.

She offers a concise yet broad exploration of a potentially confusing topic. Our lives are filled with pairs of opposites; enticing and boring, light and dark, useful and dangerous, authentic and fake. In a world where even spirituality has become monetized, this book is filled with a rich understanding of the pitfalls, shortcomings, false promises, unrealistic expectations, and warning signs that lie ahead.

Katie shows us how to tune into a fuller spiritual and soulful being in the service of uncovering the gifts at the core of our humanity and thereby build a more complete and resilient inner literacy. Both novice seeker and seasoned professionals will find an up-to-date summary of contemporary spirituality, a glossary of terms, an extensive reference list, and trustworthy resources for those who wish to nourish the spirit and soul.

It is true that each of us is on a spiritual journey, whether we acknowledge it or not. This book is an invitation to wholeheartedly embrace new possibilities for seeing where you are, where you want to go, and the recognition that there may be more inside of you that is worthy of your kind attention. In this way, you may notice an improvement in the quality of your being while you are doing your doing.

Reading this book might bring you moments of caution and surprise but mostly a more inspired vision of what lies waiting in your heart.

Dr. Allan Donsky

www.allandonsky.ca

Dr. Allan Donsky LinkedIn

This guidebook is for those who have felt the call of their spiritual path. If you have already started on this journey you may have found that a common challenge is that there is a lot of information out there, and often no clear roadmap. It is hard to know what is helpful and who is a credible source. It is hard to know what you don't know in this area. Many of us on a spiritual journey learn what is helpful or harmful the hard way; I don't believe this should continue to be the case.

I put this guidebook together because I have had my own harmful experiences when trying to navigate my spiritual awakening. I also see these concerns come up again and again for my clients. I see firsthand the damage that many popular spiritual beliefs or so-called spiritual teachers or healers can do. (I am in no way saying that everything out there is harmful. Far from it. There is a lot of good out in the world).

This guidebook is meant to be a part of the antidote to the unhelpful or harmful messages within toxic spirituality. The intention is to help you be aware of unhelpful, even harmful, messages and teachings. My aim is to help you proceed on your spiritual path with safety, boundaries, and discernment. It is not intended to blame or shame. It is a loving call to accountability and to moving forward as a community in a more integrated and conscious manner. To continue to call for an ongoing commitment to do better as we know better. None of us have it all figured out; learning is a part of the process.

I am a strong believer that there is value in both psychological and holistic approaches. We need to look at body, mind and spirit when it comes to our healing journeys. I am writing this book to help support the integration of these three worlds.

If the messages in this book resonate with you I invite you to continue connecting.

You can find me at: katieturnerpsychology.com

Tips for Using this Guidebook

The information in this guidebook is broken down into sections. You may use this book in any order that you wish. This guidebook is set up for you to skip to the section you most need at the moment, though I recommend reading the entire book. When we have an idea of potential red flags, we are better equipped to navigate them if we do encounter them.

This guidebook is based on a combination of personal and professional experience, including a combination of research, advanced clinical training, and case studies in my clinical practice. Research findings and additional resources will be included at the end of this guidebook and organized by section and topic for your reference. Case studies can point towards areas for further investigation. Please note that case studies are never a substitute for empirically validated research. More research still needs to be done in many of these areas. My intention in sharing case summaries is to open up discussion. It is also to provide validation to similar experiences. Any case studies used to highlight examples are a collection of shared experiences. These examples are based on the reports of many different individuals. The key experiences are shared and no personal or identifying information is included to protect the confidentiality of any individuals. Any similarity to your own experience is purely coincidental.

On the flip side, some descriptions may not fit or feel true for you. No one set of advice can ever apply to everyone in all circumstances. Please use your own best judgment. Take what fits and feels helpful for you and leave the rest. I am sharing the following based on my experiences and awareness at the time of writing this. I am mindful that knowledge continues to expand and be updated. The information may not fit or feel complete at a future date.

When it comes to the intuitive realm I am in no way claiming to have it all figured out or have all the answers. What I do have is two decades of devoting myself to my own path and many years of experience in supporting thousands of others as they navigate their own journeys.

The realm of the soul or spirit is beyond the realm of our rational minds alone. I don't expect to ever have it all figured out or understand it all within my lifetime. My hope is to continue to do my best, to keep learning, and to be of service. My intention in sharing my experience is to help you to prepare for your own journey. It is my wish that this guidebook can help you to avoid unnecessary pitfalls or potential harm.

Thank you for being a part of this journey.

Let's dive in!

INTRODUCTION

Before we dive into the content of this guidebook, I will share a little bit about myself and my experience to help you decide if the information included is a fit for you or not. As you will come to see, I encourage you to use your own best judgment in any content, teaching, or healing relationship.

My name is Katie Turner. I am a Registered Psychologist with a private practice in Alberta (Canada). I am also a highly sensitive person and empath. One of my areas of specialization is in working with others with these gifts. I incorporate a spiritual and intuitive lens along with more traditional psychological approaches to help my clients with deeper healing and transformation.

I want to start by saying I have not always described myself as "spiritual" or "intuitive". I was very much a skeptic. There was a point in my life where I considered these matters too "woo" to be worthy of much consideration. I believed only in science, empirically validated research, and what could be directly observed, measured, verified and repeated. (To be clear, I do still believe in the value of science).

I started out with a couple of degrees in psychology, along with several postgraduate trainings and certifications. I spent a few years immersed in the traditional mental health field. Then I unwittingly stumbled into my own spiritual, or intuitive, awakening. This was not something I had intentionally sought out or even believed in. I had not given much thought or credibility to spirituality or intuition. If it helped people cope, great. Otherwise, it was not something I took very seriously; I thought it was a placebo effect at best. The power of our belief systems, but not more effective than a sugar pill. The placebo effect is powerful, of course. It is often very impressive (Dispenza, 2015; Lipton, 2016). Yet, I did not give so-called spiritually based approaches much merit beyond this.

Reaching my own burnout and disillusionment began to change this belief. Realizing the limitations of the traditional mental health system led me to question if what I had been taught was all there was. Experiences such as overburdened systems, limitations with conscious mind focus alone, and tools that felt limited at best. I was frustrated with the number of people who were trying to heal yet remained stuck. Systems were limited in how they could support the people they were meant to serve, leading to burnout for those who they were supposed to be helping.

This calling for something different led me to seek more. It started as a quiet whisper; a call to explore other healing modalities and traditions, to question the effectiveness and validity of an individual change model alone. I spent almost a year in India and Nepal, exploring practices outside of the traditional psychology world - various forms of meditation, learning, and training in energy work and non-traditional healing modalities. I continued to explore so-called 'alternative' practices such as energy healing modalities, meditation, breath-work, intuitive development, and more.

For a number of years, I kept both parts of myself very separate. I did not mix my work in psychology with my unfolding spiritual experiences. I was very much in the spiritual "closet". I understood the medical model and the Diagnostic and Statistical Manual of Mental Disorders or DSM-V (American Psychological Association, 2017). Many of the experiences I was having could be easily misunderstood, or even labelled as "a break from reality" according to the DSM-V model alone. Woollacott and Lorimer (2022) refer to this separation between the spiritual lives of scientists and academics who have gone through a spiritual awakening as the "divided life". In their research, it was found to be the norm for scientists to only share these experiences with a select few in their personal lives. For many years I too lived this divided life.

I won't get into the details of everything. Perhaps this is for another book! It was like a trip down the rabbit hole. Experiences such as past life regressions, mediumship abilities, ancestral healing, intuitive messages, and more. Experiences that my logical mind would have had no way of knowing on its own... or even had believed in.

As I became more comfortable in sharing my experiences I found I was not alone. There are many other people who have had their own similar experiences, the type that let us know there is more to this life and reality beyond our five senses... beyond this physical world, time and space itself. Many of these spiritual experiences were more common than I had realized, in part because many people are selective about who or where they share these types of experiences, for the very same reasons that I was keeping quiet: concerns about being misunderstood or mislabeled.

I sought teachers, training and mentors along the way to help me integrate the best of both worlds. The psychological and the spiritual. I pursued different lenses and understandings to help make sense of these experiences. My rational mind found validation in the emerging research in quantum physics; findings such as the nature of reality seems to be one field of consciousness. That the nature of material reality is energy first, before matter. That we are a part of this field of collective consciousness and cannot be separated from it. That there is no such thing as time and space within the field itself. That there are infinite realities occurring simultaneously. And so much more that is truly paradigm-shifting (McTaggart, 2008; Talbot, 2011).

It was a long road that required a significant investment on many levels. The path to combine psychology with intuition and spirituality always felt like a soul calling, but that did not make it a quick or easy process. I spent a number of years gaining experience and trust in my intuition and non-traditional energy work practices. I also completed additional certification, mentorship, and training in evidence-based theories and modalities within the field of psychology. This was over a decade (and counting) of different, intensive teachings and mentorship.

For regulated healthcare professionals, interventions need to be empirically grounded and evidence-based. If you are a health professional picking up this book I am so glad you are here. I hope this guidebook can help encourage your own path. Be sure to follow your own code of ethics and standards for training and supervision.

I have come to experience that we are part of a larger field of consciousness. That this larger field is a source of unconditional love. It is part of us and we are a part of it. When we can find our way back to connecting with this source it is a place of comfort, healing, and even miracles. I have been honoured to witness the transformative power of developing this connection in my clinical work with thousands of clients from all walks of life.

The connection between this part of ourselves is the missing piece we are searching for. It is a key part of our path back to love and wholeness. I hope this work will encourage you to find this connection within yourself. There is so much love waiting for you here.

You can find more information about my areas of training and specialties at: katieturnerpsychology.com

CONTENTS

CONTENTS

Spiritual Awakening Experinces

What is a spiritual awakening and how do you know if you are going through one? Spiritual awakening experiences often refer to the direct experience of an expanded sense of reality. It is an experience or felt sense of being a part of something greater than yourself. It may be a feeling of unity, collective consciousness, of being a part of a loving universe. It can be a direct experience or deep knowing that you are loved, supported and not alone. A feeling or experience of union with a universal spirit or however you define a higher power. This is not in a rational or logical way but in a profound experiential sense. It is experiencing and knowing rather than believing at the level of the mind alone.

Spirituality and religion can be confused with one another but they are not the same thing. Spirituality refers to a personal connection with a higher power. It is an individual experience and process. While religion is more the set of beliefs and practices that are part of a shared belief system. Religion is meant to enhance personal spirituality, although this may not always be the case in every religious community. A person can be both spiritual and religious, can be spiritual without being religious, can be religious without being spiritual or might be neither spiritual nor religious. Spirituality is available to all of us, whether we identify as religious or not.

Spiritual awakening experiences can be different for each individual. The process is not exactly the same for everyone. There is no one clear set of expectations or sequence of events that everyone will experience in the same way. A spiritual awakening generally contains two elements. The first is a spiritually transforming experience or series of experiences. The second is the process of transformation that occurs as a result of the experience of an expanded sense of reality (Woollcott & Lorimer, 2022).

There are different paths that can lead to the process of a spiritual awakening. For some, these experiences may come during a time of struggle and difficulty, such as feeling a response to prayer. Spiritual awakening experiences can be the result of seeking and consciously engaging in practices to help open up to a sense of personal connection beyond one's self. While others seem to stumble into a spiritual awakening. It is not something they are consciously looking for or seeking. It can feel more like it is something that is happening (whether they like it or not). The spiritual awakening process itself may be sudden and dramatic or it may be a more gradual process over time. Survey evidence indicates that they are usually more gradual than sudden (Gallop, 2003). Personally, I have found in my own experience and in my practice that gradual experiences are often easier to integrate into our day-to-day experience. All paths are equally valid and real.

There are many different pathways that may trigger a spiritual awakening. According to Woollacott and Lorimer (2022), spiritual awakening experiences are most often the result of one of the following: 1) Those that are triggered by engaging in spiritual practices. 2) Those that occur during sleep and dream experiences. 3) Those that arise spontaneously and even suddenly in day-to-day life (and are not triggered by anything specifically). 4) Those that occur due to the use of psychedelics. 5) Experiences triggered by a near-death experience (NDE). 6) Experiences that are triggered by psychic experiences such as precognition, telepathic communication, after-death communication or similar events.

No matter how the process comes about, people often report a sense of dramatic change, both internally and externally, following the experience of a spiritual awakening. Many people report that they have a change in worldview following a spiritual awakening experience. These changes in worldview can also occur suddenly, immediately and dramatically or may be experienced more as a gradual shift in worldview over time (Woollacott & Lorimer, 2022). Many people report that spiritual awakening experiences had a profound impact on their outlook and the direction of their lives (Gallop, 2002). A spiritual awakening is often profoundly life-changing. In most cases, in a positive way.

The surprising truth about spiritual awakening experiences is that they are actually rather common yet they are rarely talked about publicly. Let alone given serious attention in our current social systems (Miller, 2021; Woollacott & Lorimer, 2022). A Gallup poll found that 41% of participants rated the statement *"I have had a profound religious or mystical experience or awakening that changed the direction of my life"* as a 5 out of 5. This was on a scale of 0 to 5, where 0 =*"does not apply at all"* and 5 = *"applies completely"* (Gallop, 2002). Additionally, 84 % of the world's population is affiliated with some type of religion and even 68% of people who are not religiously affiliated believe in a higher power (PEW Research Center, 2010). No other social phenomenon that is this widespread across the globe is so ignored by our existing medical and mental health systems (Rosmarin et al., 2020).

Spiritual awakening experiences are often navigated privately and rarely discussed or shared publicly. The main reason for this for most people is due to concerns that they would be misunderstood or even ridiculed by others (Woollacott & Shumway-Cook, 2023). Individuals often find it difficult to share these experiences with family, friends and colleagues. Scientists and researchers who have experienced a spiritual awakening report that these experiences lead to a significant shift in careers or finding new approaches that would help them incorporate new understanding into their teaching, research or healthcare. Yet the majority still did not feel comfortable sharing these experiences outside of a few trusted others and did not share them directly in their professional lives or work. (McGilchrist, 2019; Woollacott & Lorimer, 2022).

Spiritual Awakening as a Direct Experience of An Expanded Sense of Reality

Researchers such as Taylor (2018) propose that there has been a false separation between science and spirituality. Traditional materialist views of life and the world promote the belief that human consciousness is a product of neural activity in the brain. And that when our brains cease to function, human consciousness also ceases to exist. Yet this does not seem to be the case in the research and reports involving near-death experiences (Long, 2014). There is evidence that consciousness seems to go beyond strictly biological causes. The very essence of our universe, ourselves and reality is consciousness. There is evidence that points towards the very nature of our reality, on a quantum level, being a unified field of energy or consciousness. This field is everywhere and within everything (including our world and us!). It is within the very essence of the universe. (McTaggart, 2008; Talbot, 2011; Talor, 2018).

There is also evidence that we are inherently wired to be able to connect with this field of consciousness. And this connection can bring us great healing and resiliency in the face of challenge and adversity. Research by Miller (2021) has shown that our brains are designed to communicate with this larger, universal field. Her research found that those who have a strong spiritual connection had increased resilience against experiencing depression and other mental health concerns. This buffer effect was shown to provide up to five times greater protection from depression. A spiritual connection has been shown to decrease vulnerability and increase resilience to depression and other mental health concerns. Brain scans of spiritual individuals compared to those who were more focused on achievement factors have been found to be healthier overall. Enhancing grit, optimism, and resilience and also providing a protective buffer against addiction, trauma and other mental health concerns. Spiritual brains are more creative, collaborative, ethical and innovative (Miller, 20201).

A spiritually connected life is an inspired life. Where experiences of hardship and challenge such as loss, uncertainty and even trauma are gateways where we are invited to move beyond mere coping. A personal spiritual connection provides us with the opportunity to transcend hardship into a life of healing, purpose, gratitude, joy and fulfillment, thriving and flourishing. This shift can lead to increases in positive emotions, a sense of flow and experiences of thriving and flourishing, or the "positive emotions" of engagement, relationships, meaning, and accomplishments (Seligman, 2002). From these perspectives science and spirituality do not have to be separate, in fact, they are inherently intertwined.

This shift in our understanding and views of the world and the nature of the universe itself has important and profound implications. A strongly material view often leads to the devaluing of other life and resources on the planet. Yet, if we are not separate from one another, from other life or species, not separate from our very planet or universe, it means that nothing is inanimate or empty, but a living, conscious field. That everything that exists contains the essence of the spiritual energy (McTaggart, 2008; Talbot, 2011; Taylor, 2018). A spiritual worldview has the potential to transform our relationships with ourselves, with one another and with the planet for the better of all of life.

And we need all the tools we can access. A collective shift in our relationship with ourselves, one another and the greater world is urgently needed. The pressures on our world are not slowing down, from greater awareness of the impact of systems of oppression, the aftermath of the pandemic, the rising cost of living, climate change, natural disasters, and wars. Mental health rates are increasing for many populations (Jorm, 2012; Mental Health First Aid, 2020; Moroz et al, 2020). Front-line providers are struggling with included rates of burnout and feelings of ineffectiveness (Lin et al, 2023) while we help our clients navigate challenges in the world that we are also facing ourselves.

I have been so profoundly grateful for spiritual tools and insights in helping others to navigate these concerns. This connection has also provided refuge and resilience in my struggle with the questions these challenges to our collective world pose. Personally, I don't know how I would feel effective in this work if I did not have spiritual resources to draw from. I also want to take a moment to acknowledge that we are all impacted to different degrees and I acknowledge the privileges I have as an able-bodied Caucasian woman from a middle-class background in Canada. I hope to be able to use the privileges I do have to help shine a light on deeper issues within our current systems to the benefit of all.

Below is a list of possible signs of a spiritual awakening as well as possible challenges and benefits. Keep in mind that when it comes to the human experience the causes and contributors are complex and multifaceted. A spiritual awakening does not guarantee any or all of the following.

Signs of a Spiritual Awakening can Include:

- Experiences with non-ordinary and/or expanded states of consciousness.
- An increased sense of connection (with others, with nature, animals, the collective).
- Opening of intuitive experiences, abilities and/or spiritual gifts.
- Questioning the purpose of material life goals, a sense of 'if this all there is?"
- Questioning previously held values and beliefs.

- Feeling lost or like you are losing your previous identity and/or ways of being in the world.
- Experiencing varying degrees of loss of interest in things you used to enjoy as a part of this process.
- Experiencing a loss of old identities or ways of being in the world.
- A shift in worldview.
- A change in the guiding principles and/or direction of your life in one or many areas.

Potential Benefits of a Spiritual Awakening can Include:

- A connection to a greater sense of purpose and meaning
- Shift in or a greater connection to an internal sense of moral principles.
- A greater sense of peace, joy, gratitude and other positive emotional states.
- Increased empathy and compassion (for others and for self).
- Feelings/knowing you are loved and supported.
- Less attachment to roles, achievements, and material possessions.
- Less need to control others or the outside world.
- Decreased perfectionism.
- Greater self-awareness, of your own patterns and conditioning. Awareness must come first and from this awareness also a greater ability to break free of old, unconscious patterns.

- A sense of positive change in the direction of your life path.
- Greater sense of self-worth, self-love and self-acceptance and an increased ability to be your authentic self in the world.
- Increased connection with your own intuition. And following your intuition can help increase your sense of purpose in the world and trust in the universe and life in general.
- Increased experiences of synchronicity. The sense of divine or higher purpose coincides with a feeling that the universe is working in your favour o support you from a place of love and guidance.
- Increased comfort, guidance and support in the face of the unknown.
- Greater acceptance and peace and reduced fear and anxiety in the face of challenging circumstances or in the face of the unknown.

Potential Challenges of a Spiritual Awakening can Include:

- Learning to navigate an expanded sense of reality is often a process that takes time and needs experience to gain understanding and trust in the process.
- When first starting out it may feel more confusing or even overwhelming. Try to find a balance between space for discomfort and growth but not so overwhelming

that it negatively impacts your ability to function in the day-to-day.

- You may feel disconnection from support systems and friendships from before your spiritual awakening. It can be important to find like-minded and hearted friends, supporters and community. This does not necessarily mean not maintaining previous connections. It is important to have a range of social connections. Each can add important dimensions to our lives. No one person can meet all of our needs for different types of support and connection.

- If you are sensitive to energies you may need to also work with boundaries and the ability to clear and protect your energy before further opening this connection. Without these skills and ability to protect yourself you may end up being more vulnerable to the emotions of others and the energy of your environments. This is often more overwhelming and not helpful.

Developing a stronger connection to spirituality is not like just developing any other skill. It is often deeply intertwined with the connection to your own soul and personal growth. Going down this path can often lead to greater self-awareness, accountability and ongoing personal growth work. This can become a part of your life path and habits. You may not be able to go back to how things were. This can have many benefits but is not always easy. You may not be able to ignore or hide from your own "stuff" anymore. It can also be less easy or even not possible to ignore red flags or situations that require you to continue to grow. Although this growth is not always an easy process, it is often worth it in the long run. If things feel destabilizing or unsafe additional support may be required first (we will get more into this in the chapter "You are Not Going Crazy").

Reflection Questions:

- What does spirituality mean to you?
- What drew you to pick up this book?
- When are there times when you have felt a connection with a sense of something greater?
- What was going on at this time in your life?
- What is your personal "why'" for wanting to develop a greater connection to your spiritual self?
- What are your current spiritual practices and ways of connecting with something larger than yourself?
- What might be the downsides (if any stand out) to increasing your connection with your spiritual self?
- What are times in your life when you took the risk to grow and to be a different version of yourself even when there were risks involved?
- What stands out for you when you look back on those experiences?
- What are the possible benefits of staying where you are now?
- What are the possible risks of starting or continuing on a spiritual awakening path?
- What is the cost of not exploring this side of yourself?

- What are the potential benefits?
- What steps can you take to manage the possible impact of any possible challenges?
- Who or what support can help you during this process?

Wherever you are in your spiritual journey, this guidebook is for you. If you are picking up this guidebook in the hope of increasing your understanding and ability to support a loved one who is going through a spiritual awakening process, I hope it will help to demystify the process. I hope it can help to ease any fears or anxieties you might have as well as provide you with practical support and guidance. No matter where you are on your journey, thank you for being here and for keeping an open mind. Approaching spirituality with an open mind can help to decrease the "divided life" for all of us.

2

Intuition as our Direct Connection to Spirit

Increased connection to intuition is often a part of a spiritual awakening experience. Intuition is our direct line of communication to the spiritual. I like to think of our intuition as our personal compass or for a more modern-day reference, our Global Positioning System (GPS) on our path. When the path is foggy we cannot see far in front of ourselves, as it is in time of uncertainty and in the unknown. We can turn to our compass or GPS and it will point us in the next, right direction. The next right step for us, in a journey that is unique to our soul and our unique time on this planet.

The difference from an actual GPS is that intuition does not give directions for the full route in advance. There may be times when we do not even know what the end destination will be. Intuition will always let us know what feels right or is the next right step from where we are now. Following this personalized guidance, one step at a time helps us to find our way. But it is like finding one step at a time in the dark. Still, there is so much benefit from this personal guidance system. When we look outside of ourselves for what we should do next in any given circumstance we are likely to get as many well-meaning opinions and advice as the number of people that we ask. All which could be right for them if they were in our shoes, but they are not and only we can know what is right for us. In life, there are very few black-and-white answers to what to do or not to do. It is more of a set of trade-offs. And to make the best decisions for our personal circumstances we need to better know ourselves, our core values and our deeper soul knowing about what choice resonates in our minds, hearts and bodies. What is deeply right for one individual can be the wrong choice for another. We each have to take responsibility for navigating our own path.

Intuition shows up as knowing. It is non-judgemental and it is not fear-based. It is not shaming, blaming or critical. It is clear and calm. After all, it comes from an all-loving source. It is our direct connection with a larger, loving universe and consciousness. It can be a profound source of healing, comfort and guidance.

Common Myths and Misconceptions about Intuition

There are many common myths and misconceptions

about what intuition is and how it works. Below I will break down some of the most common ones and what to expect in working with your own intuition instead.

Intuition is not Real or not as Valid as Logical Thinking

Intuition is not the opposite of logical or rational thinking. It is meant to be a complement to it. It can help provide us with insights and information that logical thinking alone cannot. A combination of intuition and logic can help us to make better decisions (Epstein, 2010; McCraty et al., 2004, 2004).

That Intuition is Rare

We all have some degree of intuition. It is not something only some people have. We all have our dominant ways of receiving intuitive information. We live in a culture that tends to empathize logical thought at the expense of intuitive knowledge. This is not always the case in all cultures and time periods (McGilchrist, 2019). It is a skill that anyone can develop and increase with practice. Just like any other skill, we all have talents and abilities we pick up more easily and naturally and others that are more challenging.

Intuition is Always Right or True

This is also not always the case. Intuition is not perfect or infallible. It can be a trustworthy source of guidance and can be very accurate at times but it is never 100% correct all the time. It is also a skill to interpret intuitive information and this information can be prone to misinterpretation. If we are more emotionally connected to a particular answer then this can lead to more chances for error. It is important to use intuition with logical, critical thinking and discernment. There are times when intuition may be pointing towards something that is within you to be healed and it may not be showing you the absolute truth of a current situation. Until you are very clear and experienced in your own intuitive language and interpretation proceed with an open mind and with caution and discernment. I would advise making any major life decisions based on a combination of intuition and logical reasoning. At least until you have had enough time, experience and real-world feedback to trust your intuitive knowledge to risk higher stakes on it alone.

If you Receive Intuitive Information About Someone, you Should Share it with Them

Again this is not always the case. There are many times when intuitive information that you receive is for your own awareness. So you can move forward with discernment and be aware of potential pitfalls and dangers. People are not always open to receiving intuitive messages or feedback. Sometimes it is just for your own information and it is not helpful to share with others who are not open or receptive to this feedback. Take your time to process what is coming up for you.

Consider how the information may impact someone and how clear you are in your own knowledge and interpretations. Start slow and test the waters in a more gentle way to gain insights and feedback.

That Intuition Only Comes a Certain Way or That One Way is "Better" than Others

Many times people can discount their intuition because it does not come to them in a flashy or dramatic way. It is common to want to be able to 'choose' your intuitive superpowers, such as wanting to hear clear, loud and direct audio messages or being shown a vision that shows you the answer to what you have been struggling with. Rarely does intuition line up with the demands of our ego. When we learn to listen to the ways we already receive intuitive information we can be better at picking up on it and increasing our connection with it. It still will rarely, if ever, give us all the answers in the way we ask it to or in the timeline we are asking for.

The Quest to "Find Your Gifts"

When I first started on my own spiritual path I was so eager to "find my intuitive gifts". I now know that this is a very common desire and more often a misconception about how the process of awakening can unfold. It is normal to have the desire to '"find your intuitive gifts", as if your intuition was a present you get to unwrap and then it is yours to enjoy forever. Yet my experience and those of my clients have come to show me that connection with your intuition is more like a gradual unfolding and continual evolution of your relationship with the universe. How your intuitive gifts show up, the strength of your sensitivity and how messages come to you can shift, change and evolve over time. Be open to the evolution of your intuitive abilities and practice curiosity and non-attachment to the process of unfolding. It has been close to two decades for me now and it is still unfolding and evolving. It is an ongoing and evolving relationship with this way of knowing.

The Desire to Have Intuition Serve the Rational Mind or Ego

Another common challenge and frustration in connecting with our intuition is that our rational mind will want our intuition to give us guidance and answers in a logical or rational way. This part of us wants clear and final answers. Such as: "*Will my relationship work out? What career is best for me? Should I do this or that*"? Yet intuition does not work according to the terms of the rational or logical mind. It was never meant to be a servant of the rational mind. It is actually the master. It is about learning to trust and surrender to intuition and have the rational mind serve the intuitive mind (McGilchrist, 2019). This is often not an easy process as it takes time to develop trust to surrender control and the desire to have all the answers in the timeline of our rational minds or egos.

Learning to Listen to, Develop and Trust Your Intuition

Intuition is an ability just like any other. Some people are born with more natural gifts in intuition than others, yet everyone can develop and improve their connection with intuition with practice and intention. When first starting out, it is important to know how intuition can show up and communicate with us. We will all have one or a few ways that are our most dominant ways of receiving intuitive information. We don't get to consciously choose these but we can work with them to help increase other pathways. It helps to pay attention to how you already naturally get intuitive information (versus how you want it to come to you). Other intuitive gateways often open up and increase as we learn to pay attention to our most dominant ones. Yet the dominant strengths are the easier gateways rather than trying to work with any of our non-dominant areas on their own.

Many of my earlier experiences with intuitive guidance were from learning the hard way that it was real and reliable (from the aftermath of not taking it seriously! This is often a common experience when we are starting out. We often realize intuition is real and valuable from the times we don't listen to it, which helps us open up to the value of taking it seriously. If this is the case for you know that this is a normal part of the process and have compassion for yourself. Not listening helps us to explore real-life evidence that intuition is real, true and valuable. Most of us are not taught that intuition is a real and valuable source of information, let alone to trust it. But it is never too late to start.

The most common ways that intuitive information comes in include experiences in day-to-day reality such as déjà vu or synchronicity, dreams, "glitches in the matrix" type experiences and in the form of sensory information. It is my experience that we all have one or two dominant intuitive senses. The more we learn to listen to and work with these the more they open up. These are often easier to develop a practice around working with and checking in with as our senses are available to us at all times. There is often a profound or significant feeling that comes along with intuitive information. Intuitive messages can be clear and obvious or more symbolic and metaphorical. The more symbolic and metaphorical the more time and practice it takes to learn your own intuitive language to be able to "translate" and decode the messages you are receiving.

Potential Benefits of Connecting with and Increasing your Intuition can Include:

- It is like having your own personal compass/GPS system for individual life guidance.
- When combined with logic, it can help you make better decisions. You may be able to make quicker and easier decisions.

- Intuition can be protective, it can help us to avoid harmful situations or relationships.
- It can lead to increased trust in and confidence in yourself.
- It can increase feelings of peace and comfort in times of difficulty and in the face of the unknown.
- It can help with an increased sense of purpose and following our intuition can help us to feel an increased sense of meaning and purpose in life.
- Following intuition can help us to connect with a different worldview.
- It can help increase feelings of purpose, meaning, passion and other positive emotional states.
- It can help us to access information that is not available to our logical minds alone.
- Our intuition can be a helpful life guidance system, providing us with messages, warnings and advice and support to help us navigate every aspect of our lives.
- Connection with your intuition has the potential and the power to transform your life for the better.

Below is an overview and some more common examples of each way of receiving intuitive information. Make a note of which gateways stand out the most for you. We all have at least one or two ways that are more dominant than the rest. We also may not receive intuitive information through all of these gateways. The more you are aware of how intuitive information comes in for you the more you can start paying attention to where it is already showing up. It will increase from there.

Ways of Receiving Intuitive Information

Déjà Vu

Déjà vu comes from the French term *"already dreamed"*. It refers to the experience of feeling like you have already experienced an experience you are currently having. It can be the feeling of having already had an experience or conversation that you are just having. Such as the feelings of wondering if you had dreamed about the same moment before. Or the feeling of questioning if you have had the exact same experience before. It is a felt sense of a shift in regular day-to-day experience combined with a feeling of familiarity or having already lived this experience. Déjà vu can occur for a variety of reasons and it may be related to faulty memory storage/recollection or in rare cases may be cause for concern (Bhandari, 2023). Yet for those who experience déjà vu as a part of intuition, it is often associated with there being something important or significant with the associated experience in terms of a soul path or message. It can be a sign to pay attention, to be present in the moment.

Synchronicities

Synchronicities are a sense of divine coincidence. They are events or a series of events that seem connected to one another, but are not logically or rationally connected. It is an experience of feeling like you are receiving a sign from the universe or a higher power. Many people who experience synchronicities take these as a sign that you are on the right path. They can also be a source of guidance to connect you to your path and to give you direction and important messages. Carl Jung believed that synchronicities are gateways to our deeper internal processes and carry messages and guidance for us just like our dreams (Jung, 2014, 2023). Miller (2021) reports that noticing and paying attention to synchronicities is one of the fastest and easiest ways to have more of these experiences and receive more information from our connection to our spirit. An example is thinking of someone you haven't seen for a long time only to have them call or to randomly run into them shortly after they popped up in your head. Personally, if I notice something not logically connected coming up three times within a short period of time, my general rule of thumb is to slow down and pay attention to what the message might be.

Dreams

Intuitive dreams come in different ways. Some are straightforward in terms of their messages and meaning. It could be dreaming about something only to find out it actually happened or to have it happen in the future. This may be as simple as dreaming about a conversation or event only to have the details confirmed later. It is more common than you might think for people to dream of a visit from a loved one where they are calm and at peace only to find out they died before or around the time of the dream. Other times intuitive dreams can be very metaphoric and symbolic. These dreams can also carry important messages and guidance and can stand out in your memory in waking life. More symbolic and metamorphic intuitive dreams do take additional time and practice to learn to translate into clear and helpful guidance in waking life.

"Glitches in the Matrix" Type Experiences

These are the types of experiences where reality seems to behave outside of the normal laws of operation. It is a type of experience where *"I would not have believed it if I had not seen it myself"*. It might be an animal literally dropping off a symbol or "knocking" at our door or window. It might be lights turning on and off with no clear electrical cause. It could be an item that used to belong to a deceased loved one flying off a shelf seemingly all on its own. These types of intuitive experiences are not as common, yet when they do happen they sure get our attention.

It was one of these experiences that really solidified my path of spirituality as a foundational aspect of my work in psychology. I had been wrestling with the question of what direction to take in my career path following my own spiritual awakening. I had already invested years of time, energy and sacrifice in completing grad school in order to be a psychologist. And then my spiritual awakening happened. I was questioning everything and I was internally torn about whether to continue with the (seemingly safe and logical) path in traditional psychology or to continue to follow the spiritual call. This crossroads and decision was weighing heavily on me. Until one day I was washing dishes while chatting with a friend on the phone. I put down the soap and a large bubble floated out of the dish soap. It hovered at eve level for a moment before making its way down the kitchen, all the time staying at a steady pace and eye level. It made a right turn and then a left turn and continued down the hall. Keeping steady in its path; It made another left turn and went into my energy work/meditation room where it hovered for a moment before bursting. I had been following behind it awestruck. There was no breeze, no open window, no way a bubble should have behaved that way! It made 3 separate turns and remained perfectly at eye level, moving at the same even pace the entire time. When it burst I had full-body goosebumps and a knowing that I would not get a more clear answer to the question I had been grappling with, than this. It was the spiritual path first and foremost. I had my answer for the next step and the foundation that everything was built on from that point forward. I also want to note that this in no way gave me all the answers, there was still a journey ahead of me but I was confident that I was on the right path. In times of doubt, I would be reminded of this experience and it helped me to stay the course.

Intuitive Information Through the Gateway of Sensory Information

Intuitive information also comes through the gateway of our sensory experience. This is often referred to as the "*clairs*" from the French meaning of "*clear*". Information from our sensory gateways tends to be more reliable for us to be able to consciously practice connecting with. Therefore it is one of the areas where I would encourage anyone who wants to increase their own intuitive connection to explore. Explore or work with your top one or two dominant senses and keep tuning to these one or two senses in your intuitive meditation practice. From here others can and often do open up, but more as a byproduct of learning to tap into your most dominant sense or senses first.

Clairaudience

Means "clear hearing". People who have clairaudience as one of their dominant ways of receiving intuitive information tend to get messages in the form of auditory messages. This can show up in a number of different ways. It may be an inner voice that has a different quality and tone than your regular "mind chatter or self-talk. It may be overhearing a part of a conversation or message on the radio that speaks to a question you have been asking yourself. Some individuals can receive after-death audio messages or hear the voices of their spiritual guides or angels.

One time I received the clear initial voice *"Don't park here"* as I had just pulled into a parking space and was about to head in and get groceries. I heard this message loud and clear but dismissed it as overthinking or illogical worries. It was early in my intuitive journey and my logical mind quickly dismissed it. After all, it seemed ridiculous, there was no clear or obvious reason not to park where I was. It was a busy lot and no obvious difference from other spots. When I came out with my groceries my windshield had been smashed by a large rock. Nothing was stolen, I still have no idea if it was direct vandalism or what, but I still had to deal with the cost and hassle of replacing the windshield. That was highly stressful at the time as a broke student. I sure wished I had just listened and moved to another spot! I am more likely to notice and follow this kind of guidance now, even when it doesn't make a lot (or any) logical sense.

Benefits of Clairaudience can Include:

Clairaudience is often less intrusive or distressing than some of the other senses such as clairsentience. It is usually much easier to keep a separation with clairaudience from our own processing and intuitive information. Intuitive messages through this sensory gateway can often provide clear and direct messages, comfort and practical guidance. At times it may come in as a loud, clear and direct "voice". This is more likely in a warning type of situation such as *"stop"*, *"slow down"*, or *"don't trust this person"*. It may first show up as a strong protection or warning, getting our attention when we are not trying to look for intuitive information. Once you learn to connect with this ability it can be a beautiful source of comforting messages and guidance. With practice, we can get more nuanced and clear messages. I often work with clients to help them to connect to clear and detailed guidance, such as information involving detailed next steps and plans for highly complex situations.

Challenges with Clairaudience can Include:

It can take time and practice to distinguish clairaudience from our own inner self-talk. It is often a quiet voice within us that feels very similar to our own inner dialogue. It is important to note that clairaudience also does not always feel comforted or helpful. It will depend on what your intuition is picking up on. With any intuition, it does not always mean the words are true or should be taken at face value. We need practice and experience to be able to sort out what is helpful guidance and what might be more to point us in the direction for our own healing. This is especially the case for people who pick up on after-death-type messages. Not all spiritual energies are coming from a place of highest good and loving guidance. In these cases we first need to be able to know the difference between helpful and unconditionally loving sources of guidance from those that are not helpful but well-meaning (or not so well-meaning).

Clairvoyance

The term clairvoyant has often been used to refer to some-one with psychic or intuitive abilities, yet it is just one way to receive intuitive information. Clairvoyance refers to "clear seeing". People who have clairvoyance as a dominant intuitive sense are more likely to receive intuitive information in the form of visual images, symbols or colours. This may be in your mind's eye and is very similar to imagination but has a different quality to it. It can also show up as something in your visual field "jumping out at you and getting your attention". Often this is a type of answer or guidance to a question you have been asking or an issue you have been struggling with. It might be seeing a sign or symbol, such as repeating numbers, a feather or other item of significance, or a spiritual animal.

Personally, clairvoyant ability shows up in my mind's eye, like imagination the majority of the time. I might see a certain image when working with someone that has significance to it. I have had visions of people, places and pets that turn out to be accurate. Other times these visions are more metaphorical and take time to dig deeper into the underlying meaning. We will get more into ways to work with metaphorical images in the section on working with dreams.

Benefits of Clairvoyance can Include:

It is often easier to separate what is intuition compared

to our own processing with clairvoyance. It can be easier to notice in our day-to-day lives such as seeing repeating numbers or other signs and symptoms. Clairvoyance is often less intrusive or distressing than some of the other senses such as clarisentience. Clairvoyance can provide us with helpful and useful information. At times it can also help to confirm our trust in intuitive information, especially when visions we would not otherwise know are able to be confirmed in our outside reality.

Challenges with Clairvoyance can Include:

As is the case with all intuitive abilities. It takes time and practice to increase your connection to clairvoyant information. This is often one of the senses that most people "want'" to have and so if it is not one of your initial dominant abilities, there can be a risk of getting overly attached to or focused on trying to receive messages this way. At the expense of missing out on where your real gifts are. It takes practice to distinguish what is intuitive clairvoyance from our regular day-to-day imagination. They can be so similar that we can dismiss what is flashing in our inner sight without giving it much thought. Another common challenge with clairvoyance is that for some individuals, the images in their mind's eye can be very symbolic and metaphoric. They might get flashes of colour or rich imagery that doesn't make a lot (or much of any sense) at first glance, to the rational mind. If this is the case for you then it can take more time and practice to learn how to decode the messages so that they can make sense to our logical mind and be more helpful for practical guidance.

Clairsentient or Empathic Ability

Clarisentience refers to "clear feeling". This way of receiving intuitive information is also referred to as an empathic ability or being an "empath". People with a dominant intuitive sense of clairsentience often receive information through processing intuitive information in their own bodies. This takes the form of emotional sensations for emotional empaths or physical sensations for physical empaths. It is also possible to be both an emotional and physical empath (Orloff, 2018). This intuitive ability can also show up in the form of feeling energy in physical spaces, both positive and and not so positive. It can also show up as gut feelings or knowing, such as having a bad gut feeling about a person or situation without a logical explanation, only for your gut feeling to be shown to be correct. It can show up as body sensations such as chills or goosebumps. This is often a sign that there is something important to pay attention to at the moment.

I am both a physical and emotional empath. This means that (at least at the beginning of my journey) I would get a lot of intuitive information in my physical body, from physical sensations or even pain or discomfort to emotional energy. When I first realized I had this ability and that it was real it was like a light bulb went off. For so much of my life, I felt like something was wrong with me and then I realized that I had always been taking on and absorbing so much of the energy around me. That wasn't all mine! It still took time to learn to work with and manage this ability so it feels like more of a gift rather than a curse, but the knowing itself was a huge first step.

Personally, I think this is one of the most challenging intuitive abilities to learn to work with, especially in the beginning. This was my most dominant sense when I first started on this path. It sucked and I hated it. It can be overwhelming and can feel like more of a curse than a gift at first until we learn how to know what is ours and not ours and how to not take on what is not our energy. I have since come a long way in learning to work with this ability (and this is something I help others with). I now receive intuitive information more in other ways and not as intensely in my own body anymore. If this is one of your dominant abilities and it does not feel like a gift, know that it can get a lot better. There is hope!

Benefits of Clairsentience can Include:

Intuition in the form of a gut feeling can be more obvious and often more clear to make sense of. It is usually not metaphoric or symbolic and therefore often easier to decode. This can be a bad feeling about a certain person, situation or possible option in a decision. When we learn to trust this gut sense it can help keep us safe and provide real-world and practical guidance and feedback. Physical sensations such as chills or goosebumps can help to get our attention quickly in day-to-day life. It can be like a gentle tap on the shoulder of 'there is something important happening here, I better pay attention!"

Intuition in the form of feeling physical sensations or emotions in the body can help us be more aware, attuned to and sensitive to others in our relationships. It can also be an easier intuitive sense to access, after all, our energies and sensations are always there in our body, ready and waiting for us to pay attention to them. For better or for worse. In intuitive meditation practice, we can always scan our physical and emotional sensations, this gateway is right there and easy to access.

Challenges with Clairsentience can Include:

As I already touched on, I believe that intuitive ability in terms of feeling other's physical and emotional sensations in our own bodies can be one of the most (if not the most) challenging intuitive abilities to work with. It often feels like more of a curse than a gift. At least in the beginning, until we learn to work with it. It is like being an energetic sponge who picks up everything around us. Most people with this ability don't even realize how much of their emotions and physical sensations are a result of their intuitive ability (and strictly not all their own emotions or physical sensations alone). It can be a source of overwhelm and distress to feel everything so deeply and it can result in taking on more of the difficult emotions of others and even the larger collective. The good news is that with practice and work, we can shift how we work with this ability so that it can feel more like the gift it is meant to be. It has been my experience (in my own life and in that of many of my clients) that the experience of these abilities can shift and change over time. In learning to listen to this ability my other intuitive abilities also expanded. In doing my own deeper healing work I do not take on the same amount of emotional or physical energy in my own body anymore. It truly now is a gift but it did not always feel that way. I believe it could have been a lot easier had our culture had the right mentors and guides to help navigate this ability from a young age. My hope is that the struggle doesn't have to be the case for future generations in the same way.

Claircognizance

Claircognizance refers to "clear knowing". It is the ability to know something without knowing how or why you know it. Often without clear or direct logical evidence. It can be referred to as a sudden "download" of information or knowledge that can come in the form of sudden flashing of insight or awareness. That often seems to come out of nowhere without a clear trigger. This knowledge is often difficult to translate for others to understand (unless they already know you and have trust in your intuitive abilities).

One time in my own intuitive meditation practice, I was hit with a sudden "download" of heavier information. All at once I knew that I would be taking a trip in the next few months, that it was not a vacation, that there was a serious health concern for someone else and that it would be the last time. It felt very doom and gloom and it was not the normal quality of messages I received. When I shared this with the family members who it impacted they pushed for more information from the other parties that were a part of the message. It turns out that there has been a terminal diagnosis that was already given, that has not yet been shared (my conscious/rational mind had no way of knowing). As difficult as this time was it was clear about where we needed to be and that this trip needed to be prioritized and to happen in the timeline that it did. Intuitive information doesn't always tell us what we want to hear, but what we need to know when we need to know it.

Benefits of Claircognizance can Include:

Claircognizance can provide a sudden "download" of information, and flashes of insight or understanding can provide helpful insight into personal concerns or what we need to know to navigate a situation. It may help us "know" what the next steps are in a more practical way. This way of knowing if often less symbolic and metaphorical, which makes it easier to interpret and act on.

Challenges with Claircognizance can Include:

Claircognizance can be initially more challenging to work

with directly. We cannot "force" a sudden knowing to occur. It can also be difficult to explain to others or to back up why you know what you know. We can receive a lot of information without a clear or logical source and it can be difficult to translate how we know what we know.

Clairalience

Clairalience refers to "clear smelling" or receiving intuitive information through the sense of smell. It often shows up as suddenly smelling of an odour with no clear physical source. This often has a significance to the meaning of it. It might be the sudden smell of something associated with a deceased loved one (their perfume or cologne, the cigars they would smoke). This sense tends to be more of a rare experience and is not usually a dominant ability.

One time shortly after having to put down a beloved fur baby I woke up in the middle of the night to the strong stench of a stinky dog. The smell quickly faded and there was no physical source where it could have been coming from. My dog loved to roll in stinky things. He was always getting into trouble, he would roll in dead fish, dead animals, animal poop, you name it. It felt like it was a sign that he was okay and was happily stinky and at peace. It was comforting and humorous, not what I had expected as a message at all!

Clairgustance

Clairgustance refers to "clear tasting" or receiving intuitive information in the form of the sense of taste without a clear source. It is a sense of taste that comes out of the blue and has some type of significance or meaning associated with it. An example might be a food or drink associated with a deceased loved one. A type of food or strong taste of a mineral such as iron to convey the important message about health and nutrition, etc. Clairgustance also tends to be more of a rare experience and is not usually a dominant intuitive ability.

3

How to Increase Your Intuition

As we have already discussed, we all have some degree of intuition. No matter where your current level of connection with your intuition is, you can increase this connection with practice and commitment. Research has found that the more we pay attention to intuitive phenomena, the more we experience them (Miller, 2020). The key elements of intuitive skill building are making a conscious effort to pay more attention to these messages as well as creating space in order to slow down your thoughts in your day-to-day. This slowing down is where we are more likely to be in a receptive state to receive messages. There may be times when intuitive information comes in loud and clear and can get our attention without our conscious effort. These are often very important messages to listen to. Yet to truly develop a deeper relationship with this part of ourselves we need to make it a priority to make space for this practice. In the following section, we will cover some helpful tips and practices to help you to increase your intuition.

Crafting a Practice: Creating Rituals and Routines to Connect with Intuition

Before we get into the ways to increase your connection to your intuition it is important to first understand the importance of creating the right space and regular rituals and routines to increase the chances of this information being able to be received. When we can quiet down our logical mind chatter we create the conditions to be more receptive and aware of intuitive information. When we are first getting started in developing our intuitive connection, this is an essential step. Once our connection is more strongly established we will be better able to access our intuition, even in the business of our day-to-day life. It is important to carve out time in our busy schedules to get out of our rational mind thoughts and to connect with the present moment and ourselves. This is where we are most likely to consciously cultivate a relationship with our soul.

Learning to connect with our intuition can be like starting at the shallow end of a pool and wading into deeper and deeper waters with each step. It takes time to wade into the depths. Continued practice can help increase our ability to access a deeper connection more reliably and efficiently over time. Know that this is part of the process and be prepared to be patient with yourself and the journey. The beginning can be unclear and even confusing but if this is a skill that matters to you, then do not give up hope in the process. This is a part of it and the more we can stick with it, the more our connection can strengthen and deepen over time. Think of intuition development like any other exercise. It takes practice, commitment and repetition over the long run to see the greatest results. Aim to make space for your spiritual practices and connection with your intuition a part of your overall life and self-care routines for the greatest benefit.

It is important to have practices that help you to get out of your rational mind. To take a break from thinking about the past or the future and to just be in the present moment. This can include (but is not limited to) prayer, meditation, spiritual practices and rituals, creative time, time in nature, yoga, energy work, breath work, and mindful movement. When learning to pay attention to our dominant ways of receiving intuitive information, present moment focus is the foundational practice that every other practice rests on. Give yourself the time to keep bringing your attention back to the present moment and to practice calming your mind. A foundation of all practices in creating space to connect with your intuition is cultivating an intuitive meditation practice that fits for you. This is such an essential foundation that we will cover it in more depth below.

Another issue I want to highlight before we dive deeper into accessing intuitive information is a note on one of the biggest barriers to receiving accurate intuitive information and where intuitive practices may be unsafe. The more emotional energy (especially distressing or fear-based emotions) we have on a certain topic of inquiry, the more difficult it is to receive intuitive information. We will also be discussing more on the impact of trauma and nervous system overwhelm later in this book. It is very difficult (and almost impossible) to distinguish unprocessed, activated trauma when the insanity of the stored emotions memory is very significant. If you have a history of unprocessed trauma it may be a better step to first connect with resources for creating safety within your nervous system and day-to-day reality first and foremost. The other area of concern is if you are experiencing destabilizing spiritual awakening symptoms. Stability and safety first before further opening. With time, tools and practice we can learn how to work with and how to distinguish the echoes of trauma from our intuition. Each person's situation is unique and so a reminder to use your own best judgment and to seek your own personal tailored support before proceeding with any exercise.

Meditation

Intuition may give us flashes or glimpses into the future without showing us all the steps that will take us there. It can also be a powerful source of guidance in finding the next right step. Finding your personal intuitive meditation practices is really foundational in connection with your intuitive self.

Intuition is most helpful when it is present-moment-focused. Meditation helps us to bring our attention and focus to the present moment. Meditation is an incredibly powerful gateway to our intuitive senses In fact, Dr. Judith Orloff (1996) recommends a mediation practice as one of the most powerful tools to open up and increase intuition. Developing a meditation practice helps us to learn to quiet our thinking minds. This in turn helps to increase our sensitivity to and awareness of intuitive information.

There are many, many different ways to meditate. The key feature to finding a practice that works for you is to experiment with one or two at a time, for a few times. It can take some trial and error to find what type of practice you enjoy (or can at least do and not totally hate). In the beginning, it can often be easier to follow a guided script or recording. This way you can keep bringing your attention back to the guided prompts. The key is to keep bringing your attention back to the present moment. It is not a time to listen to audiobooks or podcasts or to be thinking about the past or future. This includes taking a break from distractions and turning off your phone or other digital distractions. It is important to approach meditation as a practice. Starting a meditation practice may be difficult or even feel worse at first before you begin to see the benefit of your practice. Find a place that is comfortable enough for you to start with. Even a few minutes a day can make a big difference over time.

Another tip is that if you are highly stressed or have a

very busy mind, it can be more helpful to find a form of meditation that incorporates physical activity. This might be going for a walk or engaging in a mindful movement practice such as yoga or qigong. If it is too difficult to sit quietly and to bring your attention to your present moment awareness, get the body involved or do a workout first to help release some of this energy before attempting to quiet the mind. Some people find it helpful to focus on the present moment while they clean or workout to help calm their minds while they move their bodies.

Another helpful practice can be turning any repeating thoughts and worries into a request to the universe or a higher power for guidance and support. Some people notice an increase in intuitive messages and guidance in response to asking for help and guidance from a higher, all-loving source. Try to keep the question open-ended rather than a "yes" or "no" or "this" or "that" response. I find it helpful to set an intention to be open to receiving insights on a particular area of my life before going into a practice that helps to quiet the rational mind. I will take a moment to connect and set the intention to be open to guidance on a certain topic or area of my life. It might be about an important decision, a relation-ship, a career possibility and so forth. Try to keep it to one area for each practice session to help maintain focus. Also, know that if other information is meant to come in instead this can also happen.

Intention Setting Example Prompts:

- Help me with guidance on (this issue that I am struggling with).
- Help me understand what I need to know about this situation.
- Help me see what is mine to heal, work on or learn in this situation.
- What is important for me to know, see or understand here?
- What am I not seeing in this situation?
- What is the next right step?
- My preference is ____ What might be an even better option here?
- What is my soul wanting to learn from this experience?
- What qualities is this experience calling me to cultivate within myself?

Try to avoid getting too far ahead of yourself when you receive intuitive messages and guidance. The logical mind loves to try to fill in all the blanks, but the intuitive mind only gives us one step at a time. An example of how I made this mistake at the start of my journey is that I felt strongly guided to sign up for an intuitive healing course. I jumped right in and signed up for the entire certification track. At the time I thought it was my answer, that I would become certified and do this professionally for the rest of my career. That was not the case. I ended up withdrawing and not completing the program due to major red flags and ethical concerns with the teacher. There were often important learnings and experiences and even opportunities for deeper healing for me in this process. This person turned out to be one of my own greatest (and most challenging) lessons in red flags in spiritual healers and teachers. This was important learning for sure. Yet it also would have saved me thousands of dollars and a ton of unnecessary stress if I had just looked more into the work or even just signed up for the first course without diving all in. If you can try to take things one step at a time and allow greater knowing to unfold along the path.

It is also important to be open to how and when guidance comes to you. Guidance may reveal itself in the moment or it may also slowly become more clear over time. Remember that intuition works on the timelines of the soul and not according to the demands of our rational minds or egos. Be patient with the process and remember it is a journey and not a destination. As it is a journey, recording any impression we receive as reviewing your intuitive journal entries over a longer time period can also help to reveal important information that we can miss out on if we only limit ourselves to in-the-moment practices alone.

Keep a Journal to Record your Intuitive Experinces

If you are serious about increasing your intuitive skills it is also important to have a way of keeping track and reflecting on the messages and impressions you do receive. It is very helpful to keep a journal to record your intuitive experience.

Reviewing this journal over time can help you see larger themes and patterns and can help you gain insights into your own metaphoric and symbolic language of intuition (Rankin, 2023). This might be a paper journal, a document on your computer or a separate notes app on your phone. Use whatever method of recording your experiences feels good to you.

Reviewing this journal over time can help us to recognize repeating themes and the deeper meaning of possible messages, symbols and metaphors. It is also another way to increase our attention to intuitive information which helps us to receive more of it. Even if you are not fully sure if something is an intuitive message, make a note of it anyway. Having your journal to refer back to over time will help you sort out what was more intuitive information and what might not have been. This uncertainty is totally normal and is a part of the process. In the next section, I will cover tips on working with each way of receiving intuitive information to help you to tailor a personal practice based on your own dominant gateways.

Exploring your own Intuitive Connection by Gateway

Now that you have set the stage with your intuitive meditation practice and keeping track of your intuitive experiences let's explore working with intuitive information by each gateway. Remember to establish the habit of taking time after your intuitive meditation practice to make a quick note of anything that stood out to you. Jot down intuitive experiences at the end of each day or within your weekly routine and record any impressions when they are fresh. Below are additional tips and journal prompts to working with the different dominant ways of receiving intuitive information.

Déjà Vu

These are some of the more difficult experiences to consciously control. It is generally more helpful to keep a note of these experiences when you do notice them. Start your reflection practice by reflecting on the times when you have experienced déjà vu in the past. Continue to make note of any experiences as you continue on your journey. This may include a sense of time slowing down, and questioning of *"Have I done this before/had this conversation before?"*, goosebumps or other sensory changes that bring your focus in the present and connection with a sense of déjà vu. Even if you are not sure, write them down anyway and make note of how confident you are in the experience at the time. You can always come back to this later to gain deeper insight over time.

Journal Prompts:

- Make a note of past times you have had experiences of déjà vu.
- What stands out for you from these times?

- What significance do these experiences have for you when you look back on them?
- Was there something important in that relationship, conversation, topic or time of your life?
- Did you notice any shifts in your sensory awareness during these experiences? If so, what did you notice?
- Continue to make note of experiences of déjà vu as they occur over time.

Continue to make it a part of your practice to review your journal entries over time. This is an important part of the process as we often gain more pieces of information as time goes on that can help us to make sense of guidance that didn't make sense at the time it was received.

Synchronicities

Synchronicities are another experience we cannot really control. It is better to take the approach of being open to noticing when they do occur and recording these experiences when we notice them. Synchronicities may increase following our asking for messages and guidance regarding certain areas of struggle or questioning in our lives. They can be like a "breadcrumb" trail to follow one sign at a time. For example, if the same book title keeps coming up around you, you might overhear a conversation, someone you know mentions it and you happen to see a physical copy in an unlikely spot. If something seems to keep getting your attention, it could be worth checking out what it might mean.

Journal Prompts:

- Reflect on the times when you have experienced a sense of synchronicity.
- Were you thinking about someone only to randomly run into them shortly after?
- What was the outcome of this experience?
- Do you keep hearing the same thing or have something come up again and again in a short period of time (that doesn't make a lot of logical sense on its own)?
- How would you describe the difference between the experience of synchronicity compared to random chance events?
- How do you feel when these events are happening?
- Continue to make a note of experiences of synchronicities as you notice them over time.

Continue to make it a part of your practice to review your journal entries over time. This is an important part of the process as we often gain more pieces of information as time goes on that can help us to make sense of guidance that didn't make sense at the time it was received.

Working with Intuitive Dreams

During our dream state our conscious mind is resting and

the subconscious mind has more space to provide us with intuitive information (Rankni, 2023). If you are a vivid dreamer you may be more likely to also access intuitive information in your dream state and it can be a helpful practice to begin to pay attention to your dreams for deeper self-awareness and insights. If dreams are one of the ways you receive intuitive information, keeping a dream journal is a very helpful practice (Orloff, 1996). Some people prefer to keep a dream journal on its own to record all the dreams they remember each morning. This can help us to learn to tell the difference between regular processing dreams and intuitive dreams.

Practice getting into the habit of setting the intention to remember your dreams before you go to sleep. This can help you to be more aware of your dreams and more likely to remember them. Wake up a few minutes earlier to be able to make a quick note of what you remember from your dreams before getting out of bed and getting started with your day. When we are first waking up, we are most likely to remember and have access to our dreams. This practice on its own can help increase our memory and recall of details from our dreams. Themes to notice include any visuals and themes, important elements, how you are feeling in the dream state (the dominant emotions in the dream) and any other areas that get your attention.

If your dreams tend to be more metaphoric and symbolic then you will also need to learn how to explore these images on a deeper level to help "decode" the potential meaning.

For more metaphoric and symbolic images practice exploring the scene from multiple perspectives. Asking open-ended questions from multiple vantage points can help reveal deeper levels of information and guidance. For example: if you have an image of a plane that is getting ready to take off and you and another person are there with luggage you can explore: *"How do I feel towards the other person? The plane? The luggage? What might each represent? What are the messages (from me, the other person, the plane, the luggage)"*? Then repeat the process from the perspective of each main element in the image: *"How does the other person feel towards me, the plane the luggage? What are the messages? What might it represent"*? This is also a helpful process to use in exploring themes with metaphoric and symbolic clairvoyant messages.

Journal Prompts:

- Make a note of any previous dreams that stand out for you.
- Are there any repeating patterns in your dreams?
- What might these represent/mean to you?
- Reflect on any times where your dreams have provided you with intuitive information.
- What stands out for you from these dreams?
- How did these dreams look, feel, seem different from other dreams?
- Have you had different themes in your dreams or repeating dreams at different times in your life?
- If so, what was going on in your life at the time?

- Practice making a note of your dreams to continue to increase your understanding of the symbolic and metaphoric language of your own dreams.

Continue to make it a part of your practice to review your journal entries over time. This is an important part of the process as we often gain more pieces of information as time goes on that can help us to make sense of guidance that didn't make sense at the time it was received.

"Glitches in the Matrix" Type Experiences

These types of experiences tend to be more rare but also really tend to stand out as clear and memorable when they do occur. They tend to not be an experience that we can force to happen. They may happen more in the beginning of our intuitive development journey. They can really shock us out of feelings of doubt and questioning and into a *knowing* that there is more to life and reality than the physical world alone. For many people, this might set them or nudge them onto a spiritual path, (like my bubble experience did for me). Once we have developed more of a connection with our intuition they may not be as common as we are listening and receiving intuitive messages on an ongoing basis.

Journal Prompts:

- Make a note of any times that stand out for you when

physical reality, nature or animals did not behave in a way that you would expect (or even think was possible).

- Have you ever had an experience that you would not have believed if you had not experienced it directly?
- How did you feel during and after this experience?
- What were your thoughts about the experience?
- What were you going through at the time leading up to this experience?
- If you had not experienced it yourself, would you have believed someone else if they told you it happened to them prior to your own experience?
- What were the resulting changes or shifts following these experiences (if any)?
- Continue to make note of any "glitch in the matrix" experiences as they occur over time.

Continue to make it a part of your practice to review your journal entries over time. This is an important part of the process as we often gain more pieces of information as time goes on that can help us to make sense of guidance that didn't make sense at the time it was received.

Ways to Work with Intuition by Sensory Type

Now that we have reviewed intuition in the day-to-day, it is time to move on to working with intuitive mediation and the gateways of our senses. When learning to pay attention to our intuition through the gateway of the senses it is important to develop an intuitive meditation practice. This is a meditation with the purpose of connecting with your intuition through your senses. It is helpful to set the intention of being open to your intuitive guidance and exploring your awareness through the lens of your senses during this practice time.

Keep in mind that in the beginning, most of us usually have one or two dominant ways that our intuition communicates with us. At the beginning of your intuitive meditation practice keep your focus on your top one or two intuitive senses first and foremost. If you find that others begin to open with practice, this is also a common experience. You can begin to incorporate the prompts for the other sensory gateways as this happens. Until then do not start with these if they are not your dominant way. You are less likely to get the best results otherwise and this can be discouraging. If you are unsure, experiment with each one for one to two weeks at a time then review your notes to see which stands out the most for you.

If it is possible for you, set up a space for your regular intuitive mediation practice. This can help us begin to drop into a meditative state more easily with practice. This may be a designed room or area of your home. Somewhere where you can have quiet and privacy or will not be disturbed. It may be in your car, or out for a walk in nature. Use what works for your circumstances. You may wish to light a candle or burn incense, smudge or use any spiritual space clearing and protection practices that fit for you. Set the intention that only unconditional loving and positive energy is invited into this space. Approach this practice with non-judgment and without expectations. Set a timer to check in with your sensory impressions and leave yourself time to make a note of what comes up, in your journal, before transitioning back to your day-to-day routine.

Ways to Work with Clairaudience

During your intuitive meditation practice set the intention to check in with your inner voice. This may take the form of self-talk. Practice noticing the different thoughts that are coming up. Notice the energy of different types of thoughts. Are they soft? Heavy? Critical? Gentle? Knowing? Make a note of anything that you notice coming up as you scan for what you 'hear' during your intuitive meditation practice.

Journal Prompts:

- Reflect on any time when audio messages seemed to jump out at you and really get your attention from outside sources. This may be overhearing a part of a conversation, turning on the radio or flipping a channel on TV. These messages come from outside of ourselves but seem to have a different quality and sense of jumping out to get our attention.
- What felt different?
- What did the audio message seem to be "speaking to

you?" What might it have been an answer or message to?

- Are there any phrases or sayings that you have heard over and over again from different sources in a short time period?
- What was the significance of this message (if any)?
- Reflect on any times when you have received a clear inner audio message. This feels like internal thoughts or self-talk but also has a subtle, different quality to it.
- How can you tell the difference between your own inner-knowing audio message and the voice of fear or worry?
- What stands out for you from these experiences?
- Continue to make note of experiences with clairaudience as they occur over time.

Continue to make it a part of your practice to review your journal entries over time. This is an important part of the process as we often gain more pieces of information as time goes on that can help us to make sense of guidance that didn't make sense at the time it was received.

Ways to Work with Clairvoyance

During your intuitive meditation practice check in with your inner vision and make a note of any images and impressions you receive. Take time to explore your images in meditation. If your visual impressions tend to be more metaphoric and symbolic (like a waking dream) then you will also need to learn how to explore these images on a deeper level to help "decode" the potential meaning. For more metaphoric and symbolic images practice exploring the scene from multiple perspectives. (Review the section on working with inutile dreams for examples).

Journal Prompts:

- Reflect on times when visual images seemed to "jump out" or get your attention in your day-to-day.
- This might include seeing repeating numbers and noticing the time at the exact same time again and again (without setting an alarm or trying to). It might be a billboard or social media post that jumps out at you.
- What felt different about this experience from regular images?
- What did it feel like an answer to or guidance on?
- What was the significance of this experience (if any)?
- Reflect on times when you have received a clear inner visual impression about something.
- This often feels like imagination or daydreaming but has a different subtle quality to it.
- What stands out to you from these experiences?
- Continue to make note of experiences with clairvoyance as they occur over time.

Continue to make it a part of your practice to review your journal entries over time. This is an important part of the process as we often gain more information as time goes on that can help us to make sense of guidance that didn't make sense at the time it was received.

Ways to Work with Clairsentience

During your intuitive meditation practice check in with your internal feelings and sensations. Check-in with your body, your emotions and the physical sensations in your body. Get into a meditative state and ask yourself *"Is this mine? Not mine? Mine and Not mine"* Notice what arises in your body. Notice any subtle shifts in your energy within your body. Bring your attention to your body and to the present moment. Listen to your body, physical sensations and emotions and not only your thoughts. Scan for areas of tightness, tension, feelings of lightness, ease, etc. Pay attention to and make note of any physical sensations or energy shifts within your body that stand out to you. This might include a sense of energy running through your body, shivers or goosebumps, gut feelings and so forth.

Reflect on how you feel in different physical spaces. Do you notice any differences in your own body feelings and emotions in places where there has been a history of conflict or violence? What about those associated with peaceful practice and higher conscious states such as sacred sites or places of worship and spiritual practice? Experiment with noticing how your emotions and bodily sensations feel and or shift when bringing your attention to a certain person, place or situation.

One of the main challenges with clarisentience is that it often first comes up in the form of raw emotional sensations and/or physical sensations and can take more practice to learn to go deeper to get intuitive messages and guidance that can be more helpful on a more practical level. It can help to use a similar practice to explore metaphoric and symbolic dreams and clairvoyant ability. Exploring any physical and emotional sensations from multiple perspectives. Asking open-ended questions from multiple vantage points can help reveal deeper levels of information and guidance.

Energy hygiene techniques are especially important for those of us with a dominant intuitive ability of clairsentience. This can include: clearing meditation and rituals Practice energetic protection practices or rituals before going about your day and energy clearing/releasing rituals and practices at the end of the day. Practice for a few weeks and record what you notice as a result of this practice in your intuitive journal.

Make it a practice to check in with your gut feeling and not just your logical mind in your intuitive mediation practice and your day-to-day decision-making. If you are considering different options check in with how your gut feels about each. Try to put aside the thoughts of the rational mind and just pay attention to your gut-based feelings and hunches. Does it feel right? Not right? If it is about a person or relationship, what is your gut level feeling and first impression with them? Do they seem charming but you just don't trust them or have a bad feeling about them? It might be about making plans, such as having a bad feeling about scheduling a vacation during a certain time period or at a certain place. Make a note of this and proceed with caution in light of any warning-type signals from your gut.

Journal Prompts:

- Have you ever had an experience when you had a sudden change in your internal emotions or physical sensations only to find out that someone close to you was having the experience? Such as suddenly getting a strong headache only to find out that your partner is having a migraine. Or suddenly feeling very sad out of the blue only to get a call from a family member who just received sad news and is struggling?
- Are you sensitive to the energy of people and/or places?
- Do your internal emotions and/or physical sensations change and shift depending on who you are around at the moment? The space you are in? Or how those you love the most are feeling?
- Do you have a hard time feeling okay when those closest to you are struggling?
- Do you seem to take on the emotions of others around you?
- Have you ever had a gut feeling about something or someone that you could not fully explain by logic?
- What stands out to you from this experience?

- How do your gut feelings give you important information?
- Have you ever had a bad feeling about something but over-rode it and went ahead anyway?
- What was the outcome of this?
- How has your gut feeling or knowing helped you in the past?
- What was the result of that experience?
- Are there any physical sensations that seem to come out of the blue and quickly pass but seem to get your attention in the present moment?
- Continue to make note of experiences of clarisentience as they occur over time.

Continue to make it a part of your practice to review your journal entries over time. This is an important part of the process as we often gain more pieces of information as time goes on that can help us to make sense of guidance that didn't make sense at the time it was received.

Ways to Work with Claircognizance

Part of working with claircognizance can be more about being open to paying more attention when it does occur. There may be times when we get a sudden "download" of information about a certain situation, person or potential option. This might be a sense of knowing the right (or not right timing of something), such as scheduling a trip and "knowing" it won't happen, wondering if you are being negative only to end up having to cancel due to an unforeseen emergency or illness. It might be a feeling that *this is not it* for a job, a place to live, adopting an animal, and on the other side- knowing that it is right when it feels right. Sometimes you just know and can't really explain how we know that we know. It is a whole body knowing and not just checking off the right "boxes" on paper. We can also work with this ability in our intuitive meditation practice by paying attention to any hunches or sense of knowing. Is there anything that feels like you "just know it" without really knowing how you know?

Journal Prompts:

- Reflect on any times when you have experienced a sudden knowing without knowing how or why you knew the information.
- What stands out to you from this experience?
- Were you able to confirm the information at a later date?
- Reflect on times when you just knew something without knowing how you knew.
- What do you just know about a question or topic? Give yourself permission to record these knowing unfiltered, you can always come back to them later to see what has unfolded since recording them.
- Continue to make note of experiences of claircognizance as they occur over time.

Continue to make it a part of your practice to review your journal entries over time. This is an important part of the process as we often gain more pieces of information as time goes on that can help us to make sense of guidance that didn't make sense at the time it was received.

Working with Clairalience & Clairgustance

As smell and taste tend to be more of a rare intuitive type and are not commonly one of the main dominant senses it can be more helpful to focus on the first four "clairs" as a regular practice. Make a note of any time when you have experienced a strong sense of smell or taste without a clear physical cause. Be open to noticing if there are any sudden shifts in your sense of smell or taste during your intuitive meditation practice and make a note of these if they do occur.

Journal Prompts:

- Has there ever been a time (or times) when you have experienced a clear and distinct sense of taste or smell without a clear physical cause?
- What stands out for you from this time?
- Is there anything significant about the smell or taste that you experienced?
- Does it remind you of anything or anyone?
- Continue to make note of experiences of clairalience and clairgustance as they occur over time.

Continue to make it a part of your practice to review your journal entries over time. This is an important part of the process as we often gain more pieces of information as time goes on that can help us to make sense of guidance that didn't make sense at the time it was received.

Additional Tips and Tools

You can also experiment with any tools you feel called to or curious and comfortable with. This may include oracle cards, tarot cards, working with a pendulum, muscle testing, or other methods.

Consider getting support, or joining a course or a practice group to add in accountability, feedback and additional support on your journey. There can be immense value in having someone or someplace that is safe to be able to practice these skills. In these spaces, we have permission to explore our intuitive perceptions and the opportunity to gain valuable, real-time feedback on where our impressions are accurate and when they are not. Working with someone or others who also have a strong intuitive connection can help us to get deeper access to our own. Finding safe and consensual opportunities to 'read' or pick up intuitive information for others can also be a helpful practice opportunity. We are more likely to be able to receive clear intuitive guidance when we are not personally attached and it is easier to build trust and faith in knowing when we don't have the logical information in the first place!

Remember to keep an open mind and to have fun with

your practice. It is helpful to keep it light and not put too much pressure on the process or on any specifics around results.

Reflection Questions:

- What myths and misconceptions about intuition stood out the most to you?
- What memories stand out for you as when you first realized that your intuition was real?
- What experiences have you had with déjà vu?
- What are times when you experienced synchronicity?
- Have you ever had any "glitches in the matrix" type experiences?
- What is your dominant intuitive type? You can take the quiz over at www.katieturnerpsychology.com
- What are your experiences with the different intuitive senses:
- Clairaudience:
- Clairvoyance:
- Clairsentience:
- Claircognizance:
- Clairalience:
- Clairgustance:
- When was a time that you ignored your intuition? What happened?
- What routines and rituals would best fit at this current chapter of your life?

- What is one small step you can take this week to continue to make space to connect with your intuition?
- How can you incorporate time to review your journal entries over time into your practice?
- Who in your life is someone you can share your journey with your own spirituality and intuition with?
- Where might it be better to keep this separate?
- Where can you connect with others who are also on a spiritual path to find community and support in the process?

I would love to hear what examples stand out to you.

If you feel called, join me on social media to share your stories and experiences with a community of others who get it!

4

You are Not Going "Crazy"

People are often hesitant to talk openly about spiritual and intuitive experiences. It is often out of fear that others will think they are experiencing a mental health crisis or "going crazy", or they may even fear this themselves. What I want to highlight in this section is that spiritual and intuitive experiences can be real. They can be, and even often are, a part of a healthy overall mental state. It is not necessarily a sign of mental illness, psychosis or a break with reality. There are already many professional, high-functioning people who have these experiences,(that they may, or may not be, sharing openly with the outside world).

I work with many high-functioning and high-achieving individuals who are in some version of their own spiritual closet. They have a strong connection to their intuition. They have experiences beyond only the current physical world and reality. Examples include mediumship abilities, connection with spirit guides, angels, ascended masters, spirit animals and other intuitive abilities. These experiences can range from frightening and unnerving to helpful, supportive and healing. This is not to say that there are no true mental disorders; there are. There is more to the *either/or* model.

There are times when it is wise to proceed with caution, prioritizing safety and stability. Before we get into the details there are a few things to please keep in mind. Currently, there are gaps in our mainstream models for understanding these experiences. Many professionals who bridge both worlds are often hesitant to speak openly about these experiences. There is a need for more ongoing research in these areas to continue to facilitate further discussion and evidence-based integration.

Experiences outside of the realm of traditional conscious-ness can bring up concerns of possible mental health symp-toms. And they may in fact be a symptom of a mental health disorder, but not always. Our dominant way of making sense of these experiences is to label them as signs of an illness or break with reality, so it is no surprise that many people are concerned about sharing these types of experiences. We have to start by acknowledging that these types of experiences can be real, valid and even healthy. I will break down some of the key points to be aware of for your own further reflection and/or consultation with your health providers.

The DSM-5 (American Psychological Association, 2017)

has very little to say about spiritual concerns. There is a very brief mention of possible spiritual concerns under "Other Conditions that may be a focus of clinical attention: Problems Related to Other Psychosocial, Personal and Environmental Circumstances. Religious or Spiritual Problems". "*This category can be used when the focus of clinical attention is a religious or spiritual problem. Examples include distressing experiences that involve a loss or questioning of faith, problems associated with conversion to a new faith, or questioning of spiritual values that may not necessarily be related to an organized church or religious institution*" (pg. 725). And this is it! It doesn't really give a lot to go on when it comes to spiritual experiences.

Psychosis Type Mental Illness as Defined by the DSM-5

Symptoms of psychosis based on the DSM-5 include both "positive" and "negative" symptoms. Positive symptoms are where something is added to the everyday experience. Negative experiences are where something is taken away. Positive symptoms can include delusions, hallucinations (often upsetting in nature), and disorganized speech or behaviour. Negative symptoms can include flat affect, loss of emotional sensations and expression, thinking, loss of motivation or ability to care for one's self (American Psychiatric Association, 2017).

Psychosis types of experiences are often scary or frightening. They often have an aspect of paranoia and have a significant negative impact on day-to-day functioning such as an inability to work, take care of self and function well in daily tasks and routines. If there is a question of mental health symptoms, I strongly encourage seeking qualified professional support. Spiritual awakening work is not something I would recommend exploring further unless, or until, the situation is stable. To regain control of day-to-day reality and feel safe in the world again, it is important for someone to be functioning well in the present. Feel safe, grounded and in control first and foremost before exploring or deepening intuitive or spiritual connections.

Intuitive experiences can overlap with some of these symptoms. They often involve awareness outside of normal everyday consciousness, sharing some of the positive symptom descriptions above. Intuitive experiences on their own do not have to take over someone's life in a negative way. They do not have to be associated with upsetting, paranoid, disorganized or negative symptoms. Spiritual awakening experiences can be a little unnerving when they first begin, yet they are often not overwhelmingly distressing. They tend not to have a significant negative impact on day-to-day functioning. You can still take care of yourself, perform roles, work, interact with others, and so forth. This does not mean that this may not result in changes and disruption in certain areas of life. You might feel different but you can still function.

Intuitive experiences on their own are not a sign of psychosis or mental health concerns (Miller, 2021; Orloff, 1997;

Borges & Tomlinson, 2016). Although it can be a normal and valid question that often comes up as our sense of reality is expanded. The connection to intuitive guidance is often a source of comfort. Intuitive experiences can often be confirmed by evidence in the physical world. Intuitive messages are often - but not always - confirmed by events, experiences or feedback from others.

It can be very helpful to connect with qualified support on your own journey. This may include the support of someone who has also gone through a similar process, who can help to serve as a guide in navigating this new sense of awareness. There is value in the validation that you are not alone. The confirmation of intuitive experiences can be very reassuring and healing in itself.

If You are Concerned about Safety and Stability

Below are some questions for further reflection as well as possible next steps if you are concerned for yourself or someone else. They are intended to help you to tease out if there are genuine reasons to be concerned.

Reflection Questions:

- Has there been significant or concerning changes in the ability to manage schedules and routines? Can you/ they keep a regular sleep and wake schedule?

- Are you/they maintaining a minimum standard of care/responsibility for day-to-day life?
- Has there been a significant decline in important areas of functioning? How is your/their functioning in previously important roles and responsibilities?
- Are your/their experiences feeling supportive, or scary/out of control?
- Less interest and time chasing material goals is common. Giving up all your/their possessions and living on the streets - not so much.
- Does it feel like there has been a significant change in your/their personality? In overall thoughts and moods?
- Are you/they in touch with a wide range of emotions? Do these emotions seem appropriate?
- Are others who you love and trust concerned with your/their behaviour or overall mental state?

Steps You Can Take if You are Concerned

If you are concerned with a loved one, try talking to them first while keeping an open mind. Be aware of your concerns and see if they are open to appropriate professional and/or spiritual support. You might consider seeking your own professional support to help you navigate the situation in an informed way. You can also check the mental health laws in your area. Most provinces and states have laws for those who are at risk of harm to themselves or others, or for those who have shown evidence of real and significant concerns for declines

KATIE TURNER, M.SC, R.PSYCH.

in mental health and functioning. These laws are designed to make it possible to seek intervention in serious cases. There can be backlash for taking steps to impose this type of order on someone who does not want this type of support, yet it can be a necessary step to do everything you can to help someone you care about. Please seek support in the process as no one situation is exactly the same. What can be helpful to one person can feel like a betrayal or even traumatic to another. It is beyond the scope of this work to provide individual advice to any one unique situation.

If you are concerned about stigma, it can be helpful to know your rights. A good starting point is to know the Mental Health Act standards in your area. In most cases, it is very difficult for someone to have treatment forced on them against their will. Know your rights. Look for support that you feel you can trust to help sort out these experiences. You can find more on this in the resource section of this guidebook.

This guidebook is intended for those who are grounded, safe, and functioning well in the present day-to-day reality. I do not believe it is helpful or safe to focus on spiritual awakening in cases where someone is experiencing a state of crisis. Stability needs to come first. Ideally, our spiritual journeys can be based on a foundation of safety, stability and support. A spiritual connection has the most potential for healing when it helps us to manage the day-to-day realities of life, not when it makes it more difficult or almost impossible to function. If you are not in a grounded or stable place please skip to the resource section to find support before continuing in the guidebook or further awakening symptoms.

If you are in a safe, stable place, let's move on to the next section where we will address common concerns with toxic spirituality.

5

Toxic Spirituality

This section will address some of the most common popular spiritual belief systems that are often unhelpful (or even downright harmful). Many well-meaning teachings can be overly simplistic and can unintentionally trip people up. There can also be issues with larger, in-depth teachings being broken down into bite-sized bits and taken out of context. I am a lover of lifelong learning in all its forms, and something I appreciate about social media is its potential to help decrease the stigma around mental health, and make learning more accessible to so many people. Yet, there can also be downsides to breaking down large, complex topics into quick memes or videos and soundbites.

For goals in any area of our lives, simple advice cannot apply to all situations. Each person and set of circumstances is unique. General knowledge can be helpful to a certain extent, but cannot speak to the nuances of each individual situation.

There are many factors in play when it comes to where we are right now, and getting to where we want to be. It may be our goals in relationships, careers, finances, or desired feelings; there is no one right way or one clear path that applies equally to everyone. It depends on where we are starting from. Our journey is impacted by many influences within and outside of ourselves. By the resources that are available to us, our belief systems, our life experiences, our biological or genetic predispositions, and so forth. There is no one simple, quick teaching that will give any of us all we need to know.

For the purpose of this guidebook, I have included the most common questions that show up in my office. These include issues with toxic spirituality, capitalistic-based "manifestation", ego vs. soul lessons, the impact of systems of oppression and privilege, the impact of being in a human nervous system and working with a human brain and just simply not knowing what we don't know. I will cover each of these in further detail in the remainder of this guidebook. The following is not meant to be a fully exhaustive list of all potentially problematic belief systems, but I hope it can be a helpful starting point.

Problems with Manifesting: Manifesting Rooted in Capitalism

One of the main issues I see in many popular culture versions of spiritual teachings is the focus on "manifesting" that is rooted in capitalism. It is important to first be able to differentiate a soul-based desire from an ego-based desire. Without this distinction 'manifestation' teachings are often merely capitalist based consumerism dressed up in spiritual clothing. Before we dive deeper, I will review the key differences between soul-based and ego-based desires. We will also review why it is important to be able to distinguish between the two.

When you take a closer look, many popular cultural manifestation teachings are often deeply rooted in capitalistic-based value systems. We live in a consumer-based culture where we are flooded with thousands of advertisements every day. Entire billion-dollar industries rely on having us believe that having X will give us _____ (*insert feeling we are chasing here*). It should come as no surprise that many popular spiritual teachings are ingrained with the very same underpinnings.

Consider teachings that empathize manifesting fortune, fame, status, wealth, beauty and so forth. There are many self-proclaimed spiritual teachings that are basically an advertisement in themselves. Their goal is selling work with a certain coach, program or retreat to help you master your "vibration" in order to get the outside stuff or results that you have been told you need.

This approach is missing the whole point. A key part of getting clear on what we want to "manifest" is first getting clear on why we want what we want. Is it a soul calling? A desire or pull within us? Or is it what we have been taught to believe we 'should' be chasing? What is supposed to bring us happiness based on the cultural messages and norms we have been born into, compared to what are the true callings of our own connection with our soul?

These types of potentially problematic beliefs can include (and are not limited to):

- That more money is always "better" than less.
- That being in a romantic relationship is "better" than being single (or having multiple relationships over a lifetime).
- That some forms of love and relationship are more valid or acceptable than others.
- That having a slimmer body is "better" than a heavier body.
- That having all the material things is "better" than having less.
- That we should have our every desire met instantly.
- That we should always get everything we want, and in the timing we want it.

The shadow side of our ego loves a quick fix. It feeds on it. And these quick fixes can help us feel good - temporarily. The problem is that this dopamine high does not last and can lead to feeling worse in the long run. Chasing the high of the next thing leaves us on a never-ending treadmill. We are never satisfied for long; we set ourselves up to be dependent on having the next thing until the novelty fades. Always chasing, no further along in our own internal well-being than before. Research has shown that as a society, we have experienced an increase in material abundance over the last few generations. Yet this has not led to more contentment or happiness, and in fact, we may be less content overall (Myers, 2000).

For any goal, it helps to examine our underlying "why" or motivation for wanting the goal in the first place. It is helpful to first allow ourselves space to pause and to reflect on if what we are chasing will truly bring us what we desire. It is an act of nonviolent resistance to question the dominant narratives that are a part of our daily existence. To commit to coming back to our conscious awareness and higher-order core values to guide our decisions. To not just go with the flow without deeper reflection.

For example, more money is often something people want to manifest without examining their underlying "why" behind this goal. It is important to know what money can buy - and what it cannot. Studies show that money does make a big difference in overall well-being when people have enough to cover their basic human needs compared to not having enough. Having access to food, shelter, education, healthcare and other basic needs of living makes a huge and significant difference in overall well-being. Beyond this, an increase in money does not reliably increase happiness (Kaheneman & Deaton, 2010).

The relationship between money and happiness is not as

straightforward as more money always equals more happiness. Money as a means to things that are important to us and to our values can help to increase happiness. Yet the degree that money correlates with increased ratings of happiness also depends on where you live in the world, cultural and context matter. The meaning we attach to money also makes a difference. Including findings such as that where those who earned their financial wealth report higher stratification on average compared to those who receive wealth from inheritance or winnings. (Diener et al., 2010; Donnelly et al., 2018; Killingsworth, 2021; Lindqvist et al., 2020).

If we are chasing a goal without deeper reflection of our underlying "why" this can lead to chasing something that may bring us no closer to our desired outcome. If we are chasing money for more peace, joy and love it will not yield the return on investment we are seeking. When we have enough money to live comfortably and then we chase more thinking it will bring us more happiness, we will likely find ourselves on an ongoing treadmill. A better investment at this stage is working on our mindset, personal healing, and growth, to help us to feel how we want to feel more often each day. The motivation for the desire matters. In fact, it may make all the difference in living an aligned life.

Ego Wants versus Soul Desires

The ego is not a bad thing. Our ego is our sense of self and personality. Our ego has both positive and negative traits.

Our egos let us know where we end and where others begin. The concern with our egos is when it is driving our behaviour from an unhelpful or wounded place. This is when we are at risk of acting (or reacting) from a place of fear. When our egos are acting from a place of fear it is often concerned with titles and status. It reinforces a feeling of separation, or us vs. them. It is motivated from a place of "should" and driven by fear and other unhelpful emotions such as feeling not enough, not worthy, superior, etc.

Our soul, on the other hand, is our connection to the part of us that is beyond and more than our unique personality in this lifetime. It includes who we are now, but is also beyond this. It is the observer in each of us, where spirit and body meet. It is intimately connected to our true, authentic self. Our intuition is our direct line to this part of ourselves. It is how we communicate with, and receive messages from, the divine within us. The soul knows that we are inherently worthy, lovable and enough just as we are. It recognizes that we are all connected and that we are not separate. It is motivated to choose love over fear and to strive to live from our highest core values. To choose what helps over what hurts.

The goal is not to get rid of the ego. We need our egos to function in our day-to-day world and lives. Our ego helps us to observe our behaviour and gain insight into our personal worlds (Miller et al., 1965). The goal is to be aware of when the ego is driving our thoughts and behaviour from an unhelpful or shadow-based place. The goal is to return to having the ego serve the soul. To have tools to soothe and work with the shadow aspects of the ego so that it can be of service on our paths.

In my own experiences with regression work it seems to be that we each come into this life with a "blueprint" that supports our soul's evolution and growth in this lifetime. This theme is reflected in reports and studies that examine memories of past lives or reincarnation (Weiss, 1988, 1997, 2005) and literature on near death experiences (Stevenson, 1980; Mills & Tucker 2014; Tucker, 2021; Kean, 2017; University of Virginia, 2023). This may be our karma or the lessons we are here to work through in this physical experience. Our souls are working on their own personalized homework in terms of learning, growth and possible potential in each lifetime. On a soul level, the learning and growth in one lifetime are not superior to another. A life of power and riches is not superior to one of poverty and struggle. (On a personal level, of course, we would all prefer one over another!). This is also why it is important to be a part of the larger evolution of collective consciousness and social change. Our evolution as individuals is not separate from our collective evolution. When we are connected to our souls we are inspired to take healing action on all levels.

In my own experience, most of the "bigger" things I was able to manifest showed up as intuitive guidance and calling first. This includes the calling to build a spiritually-based practice. I had no idea if it was something that could be done or even if I would have any clients, but the calling was undeniable (from guided messages and even physical signs in the real world). It was not something I could ignore and I am so glad I did not. Now all my major decisions include an element of intuition, including the calling to put this guidebook out into the world.

I also see this reflected back in the experiences of clients in my practice. Their manifested dreams did not come from rational mind and ego alone. These types of callings can often go against our ego desires or what our rational minds think we want. For me, I wanted to move forward into psychology, not to question my entire career foundation. After decades of work and sacrifice, I almost let it all go! There were many years when following the call to explore the intuitive and spiritual realms felt like I was going backwards in terms of career, professional and financial success. There was a lot I was called to give up in order to trust in the process. The rewards did not come right away, or easily. It was a calling I felt I had to follow for its own sake. Because deep down I knew there would be something missing within my soul if I did not follow this call. I knew that I would wonder and regret if I chose to ignore it. I had a sense that somehow I would not be as engaged or alive in the experience of my life. This knowing was enough to take the leap. It was not for the possibility of any future material gain.

This is where the individual awakening is not separate from the collective. Personal benefits include a greater connection to a sense of meaning, feelings of peace, gratitude, connection. Feeling alive and a sense of purpose and passion. It can bring energy to the individual and a shift in relationship and how we relate to the collective. There is often a call for a better life experience and a simultaneous calling to also be of service or to help the collective in some way. Not in order to get something, but to give and receive. Our old world model views life as a zero sum game. If I give, I lose, if I focus on me, it takes away from others. Yet in the connection with expanded consciousness they are not separate. Just as in our lungs and process of breathing, the deeper the inhale, the deeper the exhale. When we tend to our own energy first we have a greater capacity to give from overflow. This is not to be confused with the hoarding of resources or excessive wealth and material goods. In the giving, there is receiving, and a true calling to be of service in a particular way. This calling is unique to each individual. It may be taking care of children, teaching, or building a different type of business model. It may be living your values and showing a new, positive model of leadership. It could be in your career, in your art, or in your activism. There are countless callings. All are needed, all are valuable.

There may be certain levels of our own expansion of consciousness where we have more co-creative power to call in what we desire. Still, it needs to be in alignment with the highest good for all. These levels often come as lessons or as a reflection of the work that has already been done. The calling then is to use this increase in abundance to love your life as well as spread that love to the community and world around you. When you are aligned and connected these desires flow almost effortlessly and simultaneously.

These are sacred timelines beyond human will or control. There are things beyond our conscious control or ego-driven goals and desires. This is not to say that we cannot have what we want. It is just to say that we have to surrender the outcome to chase the desire and commit to the path. To aim for progress and growth in different areas of our lives.

We come into all of our conditions in support of our individual soul and collective growth and evolution. The soul lessons and evolution are all that matters on a soul level. Our soul doesn't care what our bank accounts look like or how many followers we have on social media. What does our soul care about? I have included a summary of common themes that come up over and over again in my own practice and clinical work.

Common Soul-Based Themes:

- To come back to love over fear.
- To reconnect with the collective, all-loving consciousness.
- To learn how to be better people: to bring the divine to the human.
- To expand our capacity to give and receive love.

- To connect and rebuild a relationship with our own inner knowing.
- To trust this inner knowing and connect with its values
- To not harm ourselves or others. (Not out of fear of punishment or getting caught, but because it does not feel right within our inner being).
- To reclaim our divine sovereignty, power and personal empowerment.
- To return to sacred power: not aggression or power over others, but power within ourselves.
- To do what is right - what our inner being knows is right even in the face of fear.
- To experience joy, peace, love, fun, and laughter.
- To release judgment, to have compassion for ourselves and others.
- To be true to our authentic selves, to live in alignment with who we really are to the best of our ability.
- To continue to expand and evolve as individuals, generations, cultures, society and as a collective.

Refection Questions:

- What goals have you accomplished only to find that it did not bring you the feelings or internal satisfaction you had hoped it would?
- What stands out for you as the difference between ego based goals and soul desires?
- What pursuits have been connected with the most meaning, purpose and passion for you?

- What is your relationship like with consumer goods and spending?
- How do you know what is helpful in the short and longer term?
- Where are the places or situations where you are more vulnerable to reaching for a quick fix?
- How can you keep growing but also practice being present and content with where you are?
- If you gave even 5% more focus to life as a journey rather than the destination, what is the first thing that would be different in your day to day?
- How can you start to incorporate this change now?
- What is your relationship like with control and surrender ?
- Can you recognize what you cannot control?
- What would you like to be different in the future when it comes to planning, surrender and trust in the journey?
- What are times when you did not know the outcome but it turned out okay (or better than expected in the end)?
- What internal and external resources and supports can you lean on and practices you can return to to help you navigate fears in the unknown?

Problems with Conscious Mind Focus Alone

If you follow mainstream spiritual advice around manifesting your dreams, you are likely already familiar with some version of the belief that *"your thoughts create your reality"*. This often comes with the encouragement of practices such as visualizing or picturing what you want like you already have it. With the belief that it will, it will then manifest for you, that you can have anything you can feel and believe in a moment. And if you don't have it, it is basically because you do not truly believe in it enough. We covered the issue of ego versus soul-based goals in the section above.

Even when a goal feels like a soul-aligned desire, another issue is the limitations of conscious mind focus alone. Even when we are clear on our goals and they feel aligned with our core values, we still need to be aware of the possible impact of our subconscious and unconscious mind (Wiest, 2020). Otherwise, we are prone to self-sabotage even our soul-based desires.

Self-sabotage can be defined as any behaviour that creates problems for you and interferes with your ability to achieve your long-term goals. It is what is happening during the times when we are our own worst enemies and prevent our own success. Self-sabotage behaviours can show up in a variety of forms for each person. Procrastinating before an important work deadline? Racking up debt we don't need after vowing to finally stick to a budget? Dating the one with all the red flags anyway? Self-sabotage is often to blame. It can show up in making poor choices that get in the way of our success or relationships, or as any other decision that thwarts our longer-term goals and is not in alignment with our core values. Self-sabotage behaviour is often baffling to us on some level. There may be a part of us that knows that we can do better and wants to make a change. Yet there can still be times when we also feel powerless to gain control over patterns of self-sabotage. When we know better and still don't do better, self-sabotage is likely at the wheel. The information in this section can help to shed some light on why this can impact all of us and how to break the cycle.

It is important to understand the role of the various levels of the mind in order to address and heal patterns of self-sabotage. Our mind is like an iceberg. Our conscious mind, that which is above the surface, is not as big or as powerful as what lurks beneath our conscious awareness (Freud,1961, 1925; Bargh & Morella, 2008; Dijksterhuis et al. 2007; Westen, 1999). Often it is our conscious mind (which is approximately 5 - 10 % of the mind) that is the one set-ting new goals. When we have committed to a change, our conscious mind is usually already on board with wanting to get out of previous habits. However, if our subconscious and unconscious mind (the other 80 - 95% of the mind) are not on board with these goals they will continue to override the best efforts of the conscious mind . After all, when 80 - 95% is up against 5 - 10% who is going to win every time?

Our mind is not trying to sabotage or harm us. Our subconscious and unconscious minds are all about protecting us and keeping us safe. They hold a collection of all of our previous experiences. From the moment we came into this world until the present day. They also hold genetic memory and, when we get really deep, our unconscious can even hold the experiences of our ancestors (Wolynn, 2016; Reddy, 2012) and collective historical experiences (Church, 2009; Jung, 2014, 2023). These collected experiences are meant to help us and to keep us safe in the world. The problem is that what was most helpful or adaptive in the past is not always the most helpful solution in the present. People pleasing and remaining quiet may be the best strategy for a powerless 5-year-old, but not for a fully independent adult.

Many popular approaches only address the conscious mind. Work at the level of the conscious mind is important in increasing our awareness of patterns in our lives and helping us with positive coping skills and goal setting. This is often the level where personal healing and development work begins. For strategies that work at the level of the conscious mind to begin to impact and re-program the deeper levels of the mind, they need to be consistently repeated over time. Think about this like going to the gym for your brain, if you only go to the gym once or twice a month you will not likely experience much positive benefit.

If the root of a pattern did not start with the conscious mind or is the result of a trauma response (more on this later), then conscious mind approaches may not be enough to really get to the root of the issue. In these cases, they may help manage the symptoms but you are still stuck in a repeating emotional cycle. This can be frustrating at best to hopelessness-inducing at worst. The predominant focus on conscious mind tools alone was a part of my own disillusionment with the traditional mental health system. There are other approaches that work directly with the levels of the subconscious and unconscious mind. When all levels of the mind are considered this can create deeper levels of change with less effort over time. It may not be enough to just work with our conscious minds alone to achieve the results we are looking for.

I am a big believer in the power of approaches that help us to work with and reprogram our subconscious and unconscious minds. In my own healing journey, I found that conscious mind approaches only took me so far. Working with different levels of the mind as well as with the nervous system as a whole can be game-changing. (I will cover more on this in the section on Mental Health and Spirituality).

If your attempts at "manifesting" your goals have not panned out you might not be using the right tools for the job. Rewiring our minds and nervous system (and therefore our "energy") is often a longer-term process. It is not to say that it is not possible but it is important to have a realistic idea of what to expect in the journey. It also helps to have the most effective tools for the job. Simplistic spiritual approaches alone often do not provide this. This is not to say that they cannot be a helpful part of an overall toolkit. Only that we have to work with our mind and nervous system and not just our conscious mind thoughts alone.

Reflection Questions:

- Where do you notice patterns of self-sabotage in your life?
- What are your conscious mind goals in these situations?
- What ends up happening instead?
- To create a new habit start with setting a SMART (specific, measurable, attainable, relevant and time bound) goal in one or a couple of small areas at a time.
- Share your goals with others to hold yourself accountable, your odds of success increase dramatically when you share your goals with others (Klein et al, 2020).
- Aim to stick to the goal for long enough to create a new habit. (This can be anywhere from a few weeks to a few months or more).
- If the above step does not lead to the start of a new habit you may want to seek personalized consultation or support to see what might be getting in the way.
- What could be the downside, costs or risks associated with your goals?

- Do these make sense in the present day and present circumstances?
- If not, practice reassuring yourself and allowing yourself to feel what comes up in the process of growth.
- If there are real concerns, it may make more sense to step back and to address these before trying to push forward. (Example: concern: If I set boundaries at work I might get fired from my job and I cannot afford that. The solution may not be setting boundaries but it might be working on increasing job security, upgrading skills or looking for other job opportunities so you can feel secure in your financial security before implementing boundary skills at your current job.)
- Were there times in the past, in your own life or even ancestral history where this block could have been protective or made sense then?
- How can you practice compassion towards the energy of this resistance while still taking steps towards your goals?
- What tools and supports are available to you to help work through any patterns of self-sabotage?

Bypassing Social Justice Issues

A major source of harm within many modern-day spiritual practices is the complete bypassing of the impact of systems of oppression, privilege, and power. If we are not careful, the issues we have reviewed with toxic spirituality can easily cross over into social bypassing, gaslighting, and perpetuating white fragility. This can end up in an avoidance of doing the anti-oppression work that needs to be done (DiAngelo, 2018; Kendi, 2023; Saas, 2020). Toxic spirituality is used far too often to bypass the real harm that has been caused and continues to be perpetuated by systems of colonialism, white supremacy, patriarchy, and capitalism.

When it comes to "manifesting" our desires, we are not all starting in the same place. Systemic issues of privilege and access to power are very real in our physical reality and 3D world. For anyone new to this work or these conversations, privilege does not mean the absence of struggle or hardship. It means the absence of additional barriers due to race, ethnicity, gender, sexual orientation, and so forth - who you are and aspects of your identity. Greater privilege means your identity does not hold you back, at the expense of others who do not share the same aspects of identity to those holding the most power (Liedauer, 2021; McGrath, 2019).

Taking a so-called spiritual view does not give us a free pass from being a part of the solution. For those of us in more privileged positions, we have a responsibility to make this work a part of our holistic approach (Shadbot, 2022). Otherwise, we are just perpetuating these exploitative systems. Our world needs us to do better. We need to be aware of the possibility of hiding behind spiritual platitudes to excuse ourselves from doing the work. We need to be aware of the risk of weaponizing spiritual teachings to excuse ourselves from being a part of the solution.

None of us are perfect in this work. (Myself included; I am still learning and I will be learning for the rest of my lifetime). We do not have to have it all figured out. It is important to commit to ongoing learning and to de-conditioning the beliefs of these systems that we have been raised in and exist in. It is not about whether we are *racist/misogynistic/sexist/homophobic/ableist (and so forth)* or not. It is about acknowledging that we have been raised in a culture that still bears the legacy of these systems of power and privilege, that they still exist in our culture and world today. We all have a responsibility to do the work in terms of bringing these beliefs into our conscious minds and awareness so that we can continue to do better. In the hopes that our social systems and our world as a whole can be a better and more equitable place for everyone.

This work by its very nature is often deeply uncomfortable. Part of the commitment to doing this work is also accepting that we will make mistakes in it. It adds to collective gaslighting if we simply brush off these very real issues and place the sole responsibility on members of marginalized and traditionally oppressed groups. As if those at the bottom of an unjust system can just "manifest" a better reality. As if it should all be on them to change the very systems that are responsible for their oppression and disadvantage. Without those at the top even being willing to look at the problem.

We are spiritual beings in a human experience who signed up for our unique life experiences on a soul level, and we are also all challenged to evolve to higher consciousness as a collective. This means not bypassing what is not okay in the here and now in the name of spirituality. It is speaking up and following your inner being and knowing. It means challenging ourselves to stay in our own power, values, and ethics from a place of love and integrity. It means holding others accountable for wrongdoing, individually and as a collective. It does not mean power, aggression, or domination over others. It means restorative justice and reparations. The soul calling is to look at how we can be a part of the solution to help 'manifest' a better and more equitable world for all.

How You Can be Part of the Solution:

- Commit to ongoing anti-oppression learning and work as a part of your overall self-development.
- Invest in this work. Invest in teachers from traditionally oppressed backgrounds. Support their work.
- Do not ask for free labour, or for members of traditionally oppressed groups to educate you or carry this labour for you.
- Support the work of members of traditionally oppressed groups (and compensate them appropriately and equitably for their labour).
- Donate and support causes you feel called to.
- Challenge yourself to speak up in the face of traditionally oppressive ideologies and belief systems.

- Learn when to speak up with love and respect, and when to actively listen and support.
- Challenge yourself to hold more than one belief system at the same time.
- Accept that this is ongoing work. That it will not likely be completed in one generation. Yet this is not an excuse to avoid doing something.
- Commit to learning about cultural appropriation in spiriutal practices and commit to cultural appreciation.
- If you are in a position to do so, put a portion of your time, energy and resources towards building the type of world you want to see for everyone.
- Commit to do your small part to be a part of the solution. Build your commitment to this work into your ongoing routines.

Reflection Questions:

- What comes up for me in reading this section/in doing this work?
- What work have I already done in this area?
- What are some of the myths/misconceptions that have come up for me in this work?
- What do I know more about now than I did before?
- How has this changed how I show up in the world?
- How can I make this work a part of my ongoing personal development work? (Example, planning a certain amount of hours a year, each year to be engaging in ongoing learning and reflection).

- Is there an area in this work that I feel most drawn to? Most passionate about supporting?
- What is the type of world/future that I want for all people?

Creating a better world for all of us requires us all to commit to doing the challenging work of deconstructing the internalized beliefs within ourselves. This is work that will continue over generations. Start where you are and commit to ongoing progress. This work will bring up difficult emotions; be prepared for this and do not allow discomfort to be an excuse from doing the work. Learn to allow and hold space for your own difficult emotions. An integrated spiritual path is not only "love and light" at the exclusion of everything else. In the next section, we will dive deeper into how to hold space for the more challenging emotions.

Bypassing Difficult Emotions: Toxic Positivity

I am so sick of the versions of popular culture spirituality that preach some version of: "*Don't focus on the negative, you don't want to manifest more of it*". The overall message is that you should have no "negative" thoughts or emotions. And that if you do, you are responsible for bad things happening to you because you have "created" your reality, not true, not okay and not helpful, we need to do better here.

KATIE TURNER, M.SC, R.PSYCH.

Toxic positivity is another form of unhelpful to downright harmful spiritual bypassing. Only looking at the "love and light" side of the human experience ignores the complexity of life on so many levels. We are spiritual beings existing within the human nervous system. We are multilayered beings. We are impacted on a daily basis by so many factors that are beyond our fully conscious control. We did not come here into a human brain and nervous system to not have a human experience. Emotions are a part of our evolutionary history as a species. Our experience of the 6 basic emotions seems to be universal across cultures and languages. Including happiness, sadness, disgust, fear, surprise and anger. (Ekman, 1972). Yet, of course there are also nuances and differences across cultures in expression and interactions (Fang et al., 2020). Emotions are a key part of our internal guidance systems. They help to protect us and to keep us safe. They provide important feedback for us. Emotional responses are a normal and natural part of the human experience (Brown, 2021). And this includes all emotions, not just the "happy" or "positive" ones.

Practicing gratitude and focusing on the positive can all be very helpful practices. Cultivating a gratitude practice has been shown to have positive benefits for our mental and physical health, our sense of purpose, contentment and life satisfaction, relationships and positive benefits on our overall social, emotional, and psychological well-being (Bono et al., 2004; Emmons & Crumpler, 2000; Sansone & Sansone, 2010). I am in no way discounting this. What I want to challenge is the push to bypass allowing ourselves to feel the full range of human emotions. As a culture, we do not do the best job of holding space for difficult emotions. We need to allow ourselves a safe space to move through the range of normal and fully human emotions as a part of living a full life. We need to give ourselves permission to feel our own feelings without judgment or trying to force them to be something they are not. We often first need to go through uncomfortable emotions and allow all of our emotions space to be acknowledged and to be felt. There is nothing inherently less than, or wrong with, any of our emotions. It is what is driving our actions and responses that is the difference between a reaction versus a conscious response. We want to aim for conscious responding over trying to control our emotions and feelings.

The goal is not to get to a place where we control what emotions we feel. The goal is to be able to ride the waves of emotion, to get perspective and space from there. To not have our emotions driving the bus of our reactions and behaviour. When we can witness and feel our emotions we can return to a state of empowerment. Emotions then do not control us in unhelpful or unhealthy ways. We can then act from a place of alignment with our core values. Feelings need to be felt, not ignored, bypassed, or suppressed. In fact, moving through our difficult emotions is a part of the path to greater connection with self-expression, compassion, intuitive awareness, commitment, freedom and trust (Hedva, 2013). There is sacredness within both the darkness and the light (Woollacott & Lorimer, 2022).

Suppressing the healthy expression of our feelings does not help us on our healing path. This often drives the energy of these emotions into the realms of the subconscious or unconscious, where they then can take on more power in a shadow-based way. Here they can end up doing more harm than good (Nelson, 2019). For example, anger can be a signal that our boundaries are being pushed, crossed or violated. That something in the situation is not right. When we allow ourselves to experience and feel anger in a healthy way it can lead to affirmative, productive action. Anger can be a healthy force for protection and good (Lerner, 2005). When we deny it we can end up acting in passive-aggressive or aggressive ways. We can feel guilty for acting in a way that is not in alignment with our values.

If allowing yourself to feel your feelings becomes too overwhelming, honour what is coming up for you. This may be a sign that more support is needed before going too deep. Please take it slow and find the support and practices that feel safe for you. Uncomfortable is okay but traumatic is too much. Think of learning to feel difficult emotions like doing a new physical exercise. We don't want to push so hard that we injure ourselves. Then we need to recover and we are not motivated to keep with it. The process can take longer and feel worse than it needs to if we push too hard too quickly.

It is not more "spiritual" to only feel happy or grateful. True, grounded spirituality is a path to realizing your higher power. This does not mean you are happy all the time. It means you become more aware and more able to witness the external world as well as what is happening within yourself. It does not mean you stop feeling certain emotions. It means you learn to witness them and how to harness the energy of all your emotions - without letting them control your reactions in impulsive and harmful ways. It means you learn to work towards mastery over your responses in the face of even the most challenging emotions.

Perhaps enlightenment is attainable; perhaps it is possible to get to a place where we don't feel the hard emotions anymore. I am not there so I cannot speak to this. What I do know is that it is possible to gain greater mastery over our emotional reactions. With time, the intensity of the waves of emotions may also decrease, yet that is not the goal in itself, it is a byproduct of your commitment to doing your work. Learn to get comfortable with your own hard emotions. Learn how to feel them and to move through them.

You are not going to "manifest" something terrible by feeling your true feelings. When we really allow ourselves to feel our feelings we can move through them and come back to our connection with our intuition and soul self. Being able to move through all of our emotions in safe and healthy ways can only serve us well on our healing path.

Reflection Questions:

- What came up for me in reading this section?

- What emotions am I the most comfortable with?
- What emotions am I the least comfortable with?
- Are there any emotions I do not allow myself to feel or try to avoid?
- What is preventing me from allowing myself to feel the emotions I try to avoid?
- What was my experience with emotional expression like in my childhood and early life?
- Were there healthy examples of emotional expression around me? If so, what stands out for me about these?
- What is my goal/ideal future in terms of my relationship with my emotions?
- How can I balance practicing gratitude and also giving myself space to feel my authentic feelings?
- How do I know if difficult feelings are becoming too much or are something to be concerned about?
- What supports are available for me if my difficult feelings become too intense for me to tolerate on my own?

Bypassing Harm: The Call for Restorative Justice

You have likely heard some version of *"everything happens for a reason"*. It can be a source of comfort in the belief or knowing that we are a part of a bigger plan in this universe. To know that even the things that we don't want can lead us to positive changes. This is part of the nature of life. It is rare that a certain outcome or twist of fate is all good or all bad in itself. There are always ebbs and flows. Change is a constant in this life. A relationship with, and faith in, something bigger than ourselves can be a source of support and comfort.

Yet this type of statement can also be harmful if taken only at a surface level. It is also not a statement that should be forced onto someone else. Telling someone who is struggling that everything happens for a reason is not always helpful and can be insensitive or even hurtful. These types of statements often come from a well-meaning place. When someone is struggling it is difficult to just be with them in their pain. Yet, that is what most of us truly need in hard moments. Someone to see us and to be with us. Holding space for the hard emotions, without trying to fix it or "silver lining" it is one of the most loving things we can do.

In many cases, the versions of "everything happens for a reason" are another way of bypassing the hard, human emotions. It is often more to do with our own discomfort in holding space for hard things. These platitudes can be used in ways that end up being very dismissing, harmful, and gaslighting. This can include cases of a child being abused, abuse histories, violence, crime, social issues, systems of oppression, and so forth. Even if something has a soul purpose element to it, it also does not excuse or bypass the real harm and trauma on a human level.

Take a harmful or abusive relationship for example. Even if it feels like a soul mate connection where we were "destined" to meet the person. This does not mean we are destined to continue to have any type of relationship with them or to remain in an unhealthy relationship with them. Even if a child does 'choose' their parents before coming into this lifetime, this does not mean other adults should sit idly by and allow abuse to continue. It does not dismiss the real pain that has been experienced.

Far too often the "everything happens for a reason" is used to excuse looking the other way or inaction in the face of real injustice. There can be a truth on the soul level but it also does not justify or bypass the real harm and trauma on a human level. And even if on the soul level there is a greater purpose this also does not make harmful actions or tragedy okay at the human level. It is not an excuse for harmful behaviour. It does not take away the need for a charge, accountability, and restorative justice (Ness et al., 2020; Zehr et al., 2020). Things can happen for a reason on a soul level and still not be even close to okay on a human one. Our personal growth and evolution are not separate from our collective growth and evolution. Staying in our own truth, integrity, and connection to source in the face of harm and oppression is in itself a key part of this evolution.

There are many unhelpful versions of the message that "everything happens for a reason". This is such a common cultural response in times of loss that I have devoted the next section to common harmful responses in times of grief and tragedy.

Bypassing Grief and Suffering

One of the most common situations where well-meaning people offer some version of "everything happens for a reason" is in times of grief and loss. It might be in the face of death, a serious illness or injury, or other major loss. This can come from a well-intentioned place but often adds to the isolation and pain that someone is already experiencing. Rather than providing comfort, it often makes people feel more alone in their pain. Unhelpful responses include insensitive responses, absence of support, poor or bad advice and lack of empathy (Aoun et al., 2018). Emotional support is one of the types of support that is the most helpful during times of grief (Cacciatore et al., 2021).

This comes up so often that I want to address common issues and more helpful alternatives in its own section. Spiritual beliefs can help provide a sense of comfort in times of loss, yet they are not meant to fully take away the pain of grief. A spiritual connection can help us to cope in the face of pain. It does not take it away fully and completely. Take death, for example; it is normal to go through a range of emotions in the face of the death of a loved one. Yet even if you do still have a spiritual connection with them, it is not the same as having the person physically here with you. Of course, you are still going to miss them and still going to grieve. We can experience a spiritual connection and still deeply feel grief for the person (or animal) who has passed.

As a personal example, mediumship abilities have been a part of my spiritual awakening journey. I am able to communicate with/get messages from those who have passed on, including loved ones and pets. There have been times when I received messages that a death was coming. I have also connected with spirits before they come in the form of a child, prior to conception - including my own daughter. These experiences have changed my beliefs about the nature of life and death. I didn't really know what I had believed before my own spiritual awakening. (And if I had not had so many of these experiences myself at this point I doubt I would believe in them!). They have been a source of comfort, love, and reassurance. I often compare mediumship ability to having a spotty network connection. It is as if your loved one has moved so far away that you will not see them in person again in your lifetime. It can be nice to still be able to communicate with them, but it is not the same as it was when they were alive. There is still grief in the transition.

There can also be times when more healing is possible in a relationship after someone's death. I have had healing connections with deceased relatives that would not have been possible while they were alive. I have had many clients receive their own versions of positive and healing messages from a loved one who has been able to make further advancements once they transition back to the non-physical. Even here, we still need to grieve the relationship that we did not get to have with a loved one while they were alive. We can have a knowing that consciousness goes on before and after death and we will still need to allow ourselves to experience our emotions. It is not "less spiritual" to grieve.

I have included a few of the most common examples of helpful responses in times of grief below.

Unhelpful to Harmful Responses in Times of Grief can Include:

- "They are in a better place/with God now."
- "Everything happens for a reason."
- Any uninvited or unwelcome comments about how someone "*manifested*" their own death, health issues, or other times of tragedy.
- "They signed up for this"
- "If you/they would just believe it you/they could heal or still be healthy/alive".
- "God doesn't give you more than you can handle."

Reflection Questions:

- What stood out for me in this section?
- Have I ever given this type of advice? What was my intention at the time?
- Have I ever been on the receiving end of this type of advice? How did it feel at the time?

- What types of support are most comforting and helpful for you during difficult times?
- What types of support are not helpful to you during difficult times?
- What is one thing I can do differently to support someone in a difficult situation in the future?

If you have said any version of the above please know that you were likely doing your best at the time. When someone else is struggling most of us (as a culture) tend to jump into trying to make someone feel better or to "fix" things. It takes learning and practice to become more comfortable with holding space for difficult emotions. Awareness of what is not helpful is the first step. From here we can aim to do better. The next section will cover tips on how to hold space for difficult emotions.

How to Hold Safe Space

This section is for those who want to improve their ability to hold safe space for another in difficult times. I want to be very clear that I am not blaming anyone personally if you have messed this up or are still learning. Our culture and society do not do a great job of preparing us to hold space for difficult emotions. Not our own, and not for others. Most of us grow up with little to no education about emotions and healthy emotional regulation or expression. Our families of origin usually had even less acceptance, normalization or tools. This type of education is often not included in our traditional education systems or curriculum. On an individual level, it is not our fault. And on a personal level, it is still our responsibility. The ability to hold space for difficult emotions is a set of skills that gets better with practice. When we know better, we can do better.

We have reviewed how trying to make someone feel better leads to shutting down difficult conversations and emotions. This sends the message that there are certain emotions or topics that are off-limits. That we are not someone who is emotionally safe for them to be vulnerable with. Often, this makes the very person we were trying to comfort feel more isolated and alone. It can put someone who is already struggling in the position of feeling like they may need to care for our emotions instead of receiving the support they need (Brown, 2008).

If you are reading this section it is a sign that you already want to do better. Thank you for being here and for your openness in learning how to hold a safer space. In the following sections, I will break down tips on what to avoid and what to do instead. Please know that it is not about getting it perfect. Effort and willingness mean so much here. These are skills that can be improved over time with practice. It is still not for us to tell another person what the larger purpose is of any life experience.

Avoid Jumping in to Share your own Belief Systems

Even if your own spiritual beliefs and experiences are a source of comfort for you please check these at the door. Aim to meet the person where they are at and to offer the support they need. There can be comfort in messages and knowing the soul-level lessons or reasons but this is something that has to come naturally and in its own time for each person. It is still not for us to tell another person what the larger purpose is of any life experience. It is not helpful when it is forced onto another in their time of suffering. We can ask if it would be helpful to share our own experiences or beliefs, but be sure to be open to listening to their response. Try to avoid coming in with your own agenda of how you want to help. If it is not something they seem open to or wanting at that moment please respect their boundaries. When in doubt there is usually no harm in asking, as long as you are willing to let it go and shift gears if the answer is no.

Preparing your Mindset

Before jumping in to offer support it can be very helpful to first get into the mindset of holding safe space. This can help us to set the tone and intention instead of going into default of trying to fix or make someone feel better. Remind yourself that your goal is to help the person who you care about feel less alone in their pain. That is it. The goal is not to fix it, and not to make them feel better. Remind yourself that during difficult times there is usually nothing we can say that will make someone feel better. The good news is that is not what helps anyway; what is helpful is someone not feeling alone in their pain. Holding safe space is what helps. Remind yourself it is not your job to fix it or make them feel better. Hold the intention that your aim is to help them feel that they are not alone. That their pain is not too much for your relationship to hold. That they can be truly seen and accepted in their most difficult times and challenging emotions. You are not doing "nothing" when you stop trying to "fix" difficult emotions. Holding safe space is actually one of the most powerful and helpful things you can do. Just being present with someone is one of the greatest gifts we can give them. Don't lose sight of this.

Practical Tools

Once you are clear that the person you want to support is asking for you to just listen or hold space, here are some tips to help you do this. We are aiming to improve active listening skills, the very skills that help others feel that they are not alone in their suffering. This includes reflective listening, open-ended questions, acknowledgment, and encouragement. Skills that show the other person that you are genuinely interested in understanding their experience (Gottman & Silver 2015; Rosenberg, 2012, 2015).

Practical Tools Summary:

- Be aware of your non-verbals.

- Give the person your full attention.
- Cut out distractions.
- Make eye contact.
- Have an open posture.
- Show that you are interested with your body language.
- Be aware of your use of language.
- Focus on listening and showing empathy. Avoid giving advice or problem solving unless it is clear that this has been asked for.
- Demonstrate understanding with empathic communication before any advice giving or problem solving.
- Practice reflecting back on the meaning and feelings you hear from what they are saying.
- Validate their experience. For example: "It sounds like you were really hurt by what they said", "It makes sense to me that you would feel that way."
- Ask open-ended questions that include *Who, What, Where'* and *How.*
- Listen to the answers and reflect back what you are hearing/understanding.
- Avoid *Why* questions, why tends to imply judgment, even if this is not what we intend. For example: "*How did you feel when they said that*"? Not "*Why did you tell them that*?" Notice the difference in tone between the two.

With all of these communication strategies, it is important to note that practice means improvement. If this is a skill set that you are truly motivated to develop I would highly recommend practicing these skills ahead of time. These are a full new set of skills and just like any other skill it takes practice and repetition to get good at them. A skilled therapist is great at holding space, but guess what? They have practiced for years and years. They had full graduate courses on how to listen and thousands of hours of experience. They were not just naturally good at it; they worked on and honed their skills to be a good listener.

It is harder than it seems at first. No matter where you are starting from, you can get better. This can include practicing out loud on your own, in the mirror, or role-playing with someone you trust. The more you practice, the more you will make them your own, and the more natural it will become. Attempting all of these skills for the first time with someone who is in distress will not go as well as when you have practiced ahead of time when emotions are not as high.

Self-Care in Holding Safe Space

Thank you for making it this far. I am so glad there are people like yourself who want to get better at these skills. I hope the tips above can help you with this. Now that you have some of the basics, it is also important to know your own capacity and boundaries in holding space. This can include what is appropriate for you to hold space for given the nature of your relationship with the person you are holding space for. This also induces what is beyond your comfort level or is potentially unhelpful or harmful for you to hold space for.

Your personal training, history and capacity all come into play here and there is no one, clear-cut answer. Self-care in holding safe space is an essential part of preventing compassion fatigue or vicarious trauma (Kyer, 2016; Rothschild, 2002). As the old saying goes, we must put on our own oxygen mask before assisting others.

This is why it is important to also be engaging in your own self-reflection work as you practice these skills. There may be certain areas that hit too close to something that is unprocessed for you. You will also need to know your own limits about how often you can hold space as well as what and who you can hold space for. For example, if you are a manager or boss it can be appropriate to acknowledge that an employee of yours is going through a hard time. You can be in a helpful position to direct them to resources and options within the company. You can help by supporting them in a way that is appropriate for your role as their manager or boss within workload expectations and options. It is not your role (and may be professionally inappropriate) for you to hold space for too much personal information. Instead, you may direct them to appropriate resources. This can be done with compassion and framed from the perspective that you want them to get the best support for their needs.

Another example can be with a friend or family member. You also need to be aware of your own boundaries, comfort level, and limits. You can have a compassionate conversation with someone and also express your own needs and boundaries. This might include asking a friend or loved one to seek professional support when you do not feel equipped to hold space for what they are bringing up. You can offer options of how you can support them and what you need from them in terms of connecting with other supports.

An example may include: "I appreciate that you need to talk about this and I want you to get the support you need. I don't feel equipped to help you in processing your trauma. I want you to get the right support and help for this. I can help you research trauma therapist options instead".

Another example may be "I appreciate that you are frustrated with (another relative), I am not comfortable talking about them in this way. I would prefer if you talk to them directly or talk to someone who is more neutral, such as a therapist or a friend. I am going to change the subject or let you go if you keep trying to talk to me about them. I hope you can understand that my relationship with both of you is important to me and I would not talk with them about you in this way as well."

You can aim to hold safe space and also know your limits within this. This helps protect your relationship and your ability to continue to hold space in a way that is sustainable for you.

Reflection Questions:

- What are my reasons for wanting to improve my ability to hold safe space?
- How comfortable am I with my own challenging emotions?
- If I am uncomfortable with or avoid my own difficult emotions, what steps can I take to first give myself space to increase my comfort with my own difficult emotions before trying to hold a safe space for others?
- Who and where are safe spaces for me to practice these skills?
- What does capacity for holding space mean for me?
- How am I at recognizing my own limits and boundaries?
- This may be situational/short term boundaries- such as "this isn't a good time to talk right now but I can be available at_____"
- These might be longer term boundaries such as "I want you to have the support you need but unfortunately this is too close to my own trauma/I don't feel equipped to adequately support you with this topic. I can talk to you about _____ but I am not able to hold space for _____."

Bypassing the Process: Quick Fixes and Miracle Cures

Our materialistic culture often promotes quick fixes and

miracle cures (Singal, 2021). The spiritual path and communities are not immune to this draw. Another trap I often come across in the spiritual area is the search for a quick fix or a magic solution, a shortcut to "arrive" at a healed or awakened place. The promise of a quick fix or miracle cure can be alluring. Yet, our healing path needs to be a part of our habits and lifestyle. All aspects of our health require ongoing tending to. We cannot exercise once and expect to be in our best shape for life. Our eating and sleep habits need to be part of our daily habits to remain in healthy routines. Our healing work and spiritual journey also needs to be grounded in a slow, steady, ongoing practice. Ongoing practice leads to the greatest transformation over time.

There may be times when we experience breakthroughs and miracle shifts. These are amazing when they do happen. They can be transformational and motivating. Yet, the downside is that if we are not careful, we can get caught up in chasing this kind of high. The challenge is to keep going, step by step, without getting overly attached to dramatic breakthroughs. Our healing journey is not linear; it is not a straightforward process. It is more like ascending a spiral staircase. We continue to come back to lessons and learning but from a different vantage point for deeper levels of healing and integration. The goal is not to reach the top, only to continue on our journey and be present in the process. There is no arrival, therefore no rush to arrive. There is evolution on the journey.

This is also not to say that committing to and investing in the right support is not helpful. There can be so much value in the right support as we navigate our paths. It is only to say that no one training, mentorship, retreat or program will be the answer to everything. Practitioners, programs, or teachers that overpromise are often a red flag. Be aware of messages that one person or program will solve all your problems or fix everything. These marketing messages often feed off the parts of us that are chasing miracle cures and quick fixes. This awareness can help keep you grounded on your journey. If you feel any one thing is going to completely transform your life (without you having to keep doing the habitual work), chances are high that you are falling into this trap.

Some areas of growth and knowledge do take time, experience, and practice to grow into. Aim for progress and sustainable habits over perfection. Think of your spiritual practice as similar to your health habits and rituals. Aiming for sustainable practice over a quick fix will take you a lot further in your journey in the long run.

Questions for Reflection: Before Committing or Investing to a Program, Retreat or One on One Work:

- Are you hoping this work/program/retreat will completely change your life? If so, what is the evidence to support this claim?

- Is it a step you feel called to/guided to as a part of your overall journey?
- Is it within your budget?
- Do you have the time and capacity to take it on?
- Is there preparation and integration planning or support as a part of the process?
- Are you taking on the commitment for a narrow, specific result or outcome, or hoping it will solve long-standing patterns and problems?
- Are you very clear on what any practitioner, course, retreat, or program can help you with? What should you take away from it? What is required of you to get the results you are looking for?
- Is there any research or statistics to back up any claims about possible results?
- Are there clear guidelines for who will likely get the most benefit? As well as who is not a good fit for?
- Do the results seem too good to be true?
- Are you giving yourself enough time to integrate new knowledge and practices before jumping into the next thing?

Illness and Death are not a Spiritual Failure

In this section, I want to focus on challenging our collective discomfort and denial around illness, disability, and even death. The tendency to over-focus on "manifesting" and "positive thoughts" can be especially harmful here. A common underlying theme here is that a spiritual connection should result in miraculous healing, and if it is not, that you are somehow failing or doing it wrong. This often shows up when someone receives a serious medical diagnosis, an injury or accident, an unexplained health issue, or even in cases of a terminal diagnosis or death of a loved one. The push to "visualize" healing your body is often rooted in the underlying belief that recovery and prolonged life are of higher value than illness or death. Yet this is not the case at all. At the soul level, the highest good outcome is not always physical healing or recovery. And why would it be? The truth of life is, just as we all come into this physical world, we will all leave it. We are all going to die one day. This truth is inevitable. (And a reminder that we still have to cope with the hard, human emotions that illness, injury, aging, and death bring up).

On the level of the soul, each lifetime and experience has value. There are some things we can control and there are some that we cannot. We may be able to have an impact on the experience of a peaceful and loving transition to death. To come to greater acceptance of our physical limitations. But we may not be able to 'heal' completely. The truth is that all of us will die one day. There is no escaping this. Consciousness and the soul may go on, yet our time in this physical body and living this one unique life experience is limited. There comes a time for all of us when the soul is ready to make this transition. On a soul level, death is not the worst outcome; it is the ending we all face in this one precious lifetime. One lifetime is not less than another based on how long we live or how physically healthy and able we are within it. When we are looking for healing, it might be from a health condition, injury or even terminal illness. "Healing" from a soul perspective does not always mean recovery and prolonged life.

This truth can be very hard to acknowledge, let alone to accept. This does not mean we should bypass the very real and difficult human emotions. Of course, our human selves can and do face a range of emotions. Our preference for ourselves and our loved ones is a full recovery, more time, and a long lifetime. This is real and the soul level does not take this away nor is it meant to (as we covered in the section on bypassing hard emotions). I don't mean this to be discouraging and this is in no way an argument to just 'give up'. I am not promoting just giving up or accepting conditions that you are not happy with. I strongly believe in the power of commitment to our own personal awakening and healing journey, no matter what conditions are showing up in our lives. Miracles may be possible, and there are cases of miraculous healing. But there is also a danger in promoting this as the right outcome. It implies that if someone does not spontaneously recover they are somehow "failing". That they are not doing it right or not keeping their thoughts "positive enough". It sends the message that it is our choice to make when it is far, far more complcx than this.

On the level of the soul, each lifetime and experience has value. There are some things we can control and there are some that we cannot. We may be able to have an impact on the experience of a peaceful and loving transition to death or acceptance of our physical limitations, but they may not be able to "heal" completely. Even if miracles may be possible there is also a danger in promoting the belief that if someone does not spontaneously recover they are somehow "failing/ not doing it right/not being positive enough". It just may not be a part of their unique soul path.

Our culture does not do a very good job of preparing us to honour the sacred transitions of aging, illness and death. On a personal level, we can wrestle with difficult emotions with these transitions and losses. This is normal and a part of giving ourselves space to feel all our emotions, including our grief, anger, sadness, despair, and any other emotions (Jenkinson, 2015, Yalom, 2009) . The tendency for some spiritual belief systems to overly focus on "manifesting'"and only thinking positive thoughts can be especially harmful when someone is in the middle of processing a devastating diagnosis, injury, illness, or death.

I have included tips on supporting someone you care about during serious illness or grief and loss below. May it help you to bridge the practice of holding both the humans and the divine in your communication and relationships.

Supporting Someone You Care About

- Remember to get into the mindset of holding space versus trying to fix the situation.
- Aim to just be there.
- Practice your active listening skills.
- Have your own outside support and tools to help you in navigating your own feelings. With any difficult topic, the more comfortable we are to go into it ourselves, the more we increase our capacity to hold space.
- Engage in your own self-reflection. If we avoid thinking about illness or death in our own lives then our own discomfort will likely be a roadblock.
- Ask yourself if the person you want to support asked you for suggestions with manifestation, healing, or any advice you wish to offer.
- If they are not asking, ask what they might need, and offer options of ways you can support them.
- Always ask.
- Leave room for people to change what they need and to communicate this to you. What type of support is helpful can change over time or even daily.
- Do not send them articles or ask if they have tried *x,y, or z* without first making sure this would actually be experienced as helpful for them.
- When in doubt, ask and be open to listening.
- Respect their answers even if you disagree or it is hard to hear.
- Know that there is no one right way to grieve. People process in their own ways and timelines.

- If you are concerned about someone you care about, bring up your concerns in a loving way. Come from a place of checking in with them but not assuming that you know better than they do.
- Be prepared to listen to them and how they feel they are doing/what they need.

I cannot stress enough the healing power and value of just being able to be a safe space for someone who is facing something that can be so scary. It is a gift to be able to just be honest with our real feelings. These are some of the most isolating situations that many people can face.

Reflection Questions:

- What are my own feelings about aging, illness and death?
- What are my own experiences with grief and loss?
- What are the rituals and teachings around loss and death in my own family and culture of origin?
- What rituals and teachings around grieving loss and death transitions have I adopted in my own practices/ that feel right or make the most sense for me now?
- What was I taught about death and what may happen before or after death?
- Do these teachings resonate with me now?
- What thoughts and feelings come up when I think about death? My own? My loved ones?
- What experiences (if any) have I had regarding the

nature of consciousness, after death communication or spiritual experiences around death?
- What will mean the most to me at the end of my life?
- How do I want to be remembered?

What is Not Yours to Control

Another red flag in spiritual teachings is any version of messages that tell you to not reflect on real-world feedback. From actively ignoring real-world feedback from others who care about you to trying to control another person. I will touch on both in greater detail below.

Red Flag: Ignoring Real-World Feedback

This can include messages such as "visualize" the outcome/interaction you want and ignore or do not give attention to what you don't want. Taken too far, this promotes active gaslighting dressed up as "spirituality". I once saw a video on social media of some so-called spiritual practitioner recommending ignoring what your partner is telling you about concerns in your relationship. Her suggestion was to instead repeat in your mind that you have a wonderful loving relationship - while they are talking to you, to not even listen to them! Would you want to be in a relationship with someone who did this while you were trying to have a real heart-to-heart? No thank-you! This type of behaviour will lead to emotional distance or to a break-up. It is an immature

KATIE TURNER, M.SC, R.PSYCH.

and unhealthy response. Being able to reflect on feedback and change our behaviour as a result is a sign of emotional maturity and a foundational skill for healthy, mature relationships (Gibson, 2015; Goleman, 2005; Moulton Sarkis, 2018).

Take a work situation, for example; if your supervisor sits you down to go over areas for improvement, it is important to reflect on if you can see any truth to what they are saying. An example might be showing up late or not delivering on important projects. You can try to ignore your current reality because you don't like how it feels and instead just focus on visualizing the career you want. But at the end of the day, this is not helpful for you long term. Give yourself space to care for your emotions. Take the time to reflect if there is any truth to the feedback. If there is, you need to take steps to work on yourself to address the issues. This may mean engaging in self-development work or seeking outside support. It can feel pretty crappy to realize when we are screwing up, but guess what - it is supposed to feel bad. The crappy feelings are for us to pay attention to and to help motivate our behaviour so that we can and will feel better in the future.

If people who care about us are giving us feedback about something we did that was harmful we should not ignore it. This is not how "creating your own reality" works. This can be avoiding reality. There are times when the key to getting where we want to be is in being open to listen to (and take action on addressing) difficult feedback. Practicing the skills of self-awareness, self-regulation, and accountability is part of being a mature and healthy adult. This type of discomfort helps us to grow and ultimately can serve us in having the life we desire.

Red Flag: Claims of Controlling Others

I would be highly skeptical of (and would run the other way from) working with anyone who claims they can control the free will of another person. This is highly unethical and problematic. It is also not true. This person is not working from integrity and it is not an energy you want to put out into the world. They are feeding off the fears and wounds of their clients. There are many so-called readers or healers who hook people in with claims that they can get someone to fall in love with you, get your ex back, or so forth. This is a major, major red flag. Anytime we try to control another's behaviour we are getting into shady territory.

The thing is that you do not need to control anyone outside of yourself to have the peace and happiness you deserve. This can only come from within to be solid and secure. Others can be a part of this process but not a substitute for you doing your own work to arrive at this place within yourself. Our challenge in our spiritual path is to get clear on what we want and to take steps to bring ourselves closer to this (both internally and externally). Our invitation is to hold the vision of what we want while also releasing our attachment to the how, the when, and exactly what it looks like. We have to remain open to the mysteries of life. Our challenge is to take responsibility for ourselves and to also to trust in the process of surrendering what we cannot control (Orloff, 2015; Singer, 2015).

A common example is wanting a loving relationship. If you are currently in a relationship and some issues are not working it is not our job to change our partner. It is our job to work on our own side of the street. If they are willing to do the work with us, all the better. Our job is to learn to regulate ourselves better and commit to our own healing and growth. To learn about relationship dynamics and learn healthier ways to communicate and approach conflict. To practice these strategies until they become easier. We can only control our side of the street, not the other person and not the fate of the relationship itself.

It is about learning what we can influence, what is not ours to control, and releasing what is not ours to change. In the question of when to stay or leave a relationship, a few possible paths are possible. (Again, the ultimate path is a co-creation of both parties within the relationship). You may transform your relationship by changing your own patterns. This might be enough to get the relationship you desire. Your own work may make enough of a difference for you to have the relationship you desire.

Alternatively, you may come to see that your partner is not doing the work they need to do. It might not be possible to create a healthy partnership together if they remain unwilling to do their own work. When your side of the street is cleaner it becomes easier to see what was your part and what was your partner's. You may have to have some hard discussions to see if they are willing to change or grow. You may also need to continue to do your own work to see if you can make peace with the relationship as it is if they are not willing to change.

You may come to a place where you know you have done everything you can, and that you cannot be at peace or the best version of yourself if you remain in the relationship as it is. From here you may need to release the relationship in its present form. This may mean ending the relationship or renegotiating the relationship agreements. Each situation is unique and there is no one right answer. The importance is that this decision comes from a place of knowing, acceptance, and surrender. It is not up to you to force your partner to change. It is your job to know your own core needs and boundaries. What you can control and what you cannot. To communicate your needs with as much love and respect as you can, while also remaining grounded in your core needs and values. There is nothing wrong with holding a preference; this is totally normal and is not harmful in itself. The problem comes if we are holding so tightly to what we want that we slide into trying to control what is not ours to control. No matter what the outcome, when we know we have done everything we can and where we truly stand, we can move into our future without regrets. With a stronger foundation of self-awareness and personal empowerment.

When we hold to our values and the vision of the future we prefer we cannot force anyone else to change or to be different. We have to remain open and willing to see reality as it is. From here we are in a more clear position to know what we can change and what we cannot. and to make decisions in alignment. When we focus on our side of the street we can find that our path to healing and freedom is in our own hands.

Reflection Questions:

- What came up for me in this section?
- Do I tend to be more vulnerable to only looking at my own behaviour (and not holding others accountable for theirs)? If so, what do I notice about this pattern?
- Do I tend to be more vulnerable to trying to control others? If so, what do I notice about this pattern?
- When am I more prone to go into these ways of coping?
- How can I practice taking an outside/neutral observer perspective?
- What is my responsibility or for me to work on?
- What is not mine to control?
- How can I keep coming back to this difference?
- If I am unclear, who and where can help me to gain a safe and unbiased perspective of the situation?

Reality is Not a Mirror

In most situations where we are not happy with the results it is helpful to first reflect on our possible contribution to the situation. This includes our actions, behaviours, thoughts, patterns, communication style, and so forth. For example, if we are unhappy with communication in a relationship, a helpful first step is to look at our side in the interactions. If we start off our communication being aggressive or passive-aggressive the conversation is not likely to go well. If we are overly defensive this often leads to defensiveness or shutting down from the other person.

It is important to be open to reflecting on and taking accountability for our own side of the street. There are key skills we all need to develop and practice within ourselves to have more healthy and satisfying relationships: skills such as self-awareness, self-regulation, healthy communication skills, and the ability to apologize and repair. We cannot have a healthy relationship with someone else if we are not working towards healthy patterns ourselves. We also do not have to be fully healed. That is not possible. A safe relationship can be a wonderful container for growth and healing provided both partners are doing the work (Aiyana, 2002; Gottman, 2015; Johnson, 2008, 2015).

This section is for those who are already doing their own work and taking accountability for their own behaviour. It is for those who are already open to feedback from others and who work towards incorporating this feedback and doing better. These are wonderful traits to have, in most situations. Yet being too willing to take in any and all feedback can also be a problem under certain circumstances, such as if you are tolerating unacceptable or abusive behaviour from others.

There have been so many times in my work where some version of the belief "*What part of me is this person reflecting for me*" comes up. This often traces back to messages such as what you are seeing in your external world is a reflection of what you need to heal within yourself.

It often shows up as a question along the lines of "*I had this hard experience with this person and I want to see where I am being ___ *" *(the way they treated me)*. The main issue with this type of spiritual belief is that people can take it as a black-and-white truth. If you are being treated in an unacceptable or abusive way it is not helpful to ask "*What did I do to manifest this? What part of me is abusive, angry, etc.?*"

If you are already working on yourself then it is unlikely that you need to work on the exact same traits within yourself. It is usually more helpful to look at your tendencies toward setting and holding boundaries. A simple perspective shift is to take yourself out of the picture and think about if this was happening to a friend or loved one. If they were being treated this way, how would this change how you see the situation? What would you want for them in the same circumstances?

Bringing yourself into an observer perspective can help bring you into a more neutral and realistic view of the situation.

If your friend was acting poorly and someone matched their energy you can see as an observer that the interaction was not great on both sides. You would see that your friend could also benefit from learning to communicate in a more productive way. The other person could work on not responding in such a reactive way as well. They both can work on their side of the street. On the other hand, it can also make it crystal clear that your friend or loved one did not deserve to be treated or spoken to in the way they were. That it was clearly an issue with the other party. In these cases, you are likely dealing with the other person's capacity limitations in their communication with you.

Our realities have a rich amount of information reflecting back to us. It is not so simple or straightforward as *"When I see X in the world, where I am the same"*? Examples: "When I see anger, where I am angry?" When I see abuse, where am I being abusive? Selfish? Greedy? Dishonest? and so on. This is far too oversimplified.

There is potential and opportunity for growth. Be open to engaging in your own exploration. Explore more open-ended questions and reflection.

Reflection Questions to Assist you in Open-Ended Exploration:

(*The following does not apply to abusive or unsafe situations).

- Have I done the work to be aware of my own part of the communication dynamics?
- If this dynamic was happening to a loved one, how would I see the situation differently?
- What is my responsibility?
- What is the other person's responsibility?
- Is this a communication issue or a boundary issue?
- How can I set better boundaries, speak up, and focus on what I can control in a way that feels right for me?
- What does this type of interaction/communication dynamic bring up for me?
- Does it remind me of any earlier dynamics in my life?
- What response comes up for me? (For example: Do I try to keep the peace, placate, do I go into guilt and try to "make it right" even when I logically know I did nothing wrong? Do I feel powerless? Do I shut down? Do I become passive-aggressive?
- What areas am I being called to grow in with this situation?

This type of self-reflection can help us to access our own subconscious and unconscious patterns that we may not otherwise be aware of. This type of self-exploration can lead to valuable insights, healing and growth.

Planifesting over Manifesting

I have seen far too many spiritual people end up stuck for far too long (or end up in unwanted situations) due to not putting enough energy into a practical plan. They pour energy into working in the energetic realm, yet do not take any real-world steps toward their dreams. All the visualization in the world cannot get you where you want to go on its own. There is also the need for inspired action. Or sometimes, just some kind of action. A simple step to move away from what you don't want. We live in an energetic as well as a physical world. The energetic may be the building blocks of the physical, yet both are important. Dr. Orloff (1996) also recommends taking a balanced approach to intuition in everyday life, by striving for a healthy balance between intuitive processing and taking steps within your best efforts to meet the requirements of life. The spiritual can be a helpful and healing connection but practice balance by also taking steps in day to day life.

Instead of "manifesting" I am a much bigger fan of the term planifesting. Planifesting goes beyond just visualizing the future you want. It takes clarity on the desired future further, to also break down our vision into goals and steps to help bring our goals into reality. There is still space for spiritual practices such as medication and visualization. There is still room to be open to the unexpected opportunities and blessings that can come our way in the process. Planifesting calls for a blend of intuition and logic. It is where having faith and moving your feet meet.

The first step is getting clear on your most meaningful

goal. Allow yourself space to explore what goals are the most important to you at this stage of your life. To start with this might be carving out some time from your other commitments to create time for exploration. Allow yourself to journal, to daydream, to research options. Let your imagination run wild. Planning will be for later.

Once you are more clear on what goal is most important to you, start to look at how you might be able to get there from where you are now. Aim for SMART goals: specific, measurable, attainable, relevant, and time-bound. Be realistic and compassionate with yourself about what is sustainable. Aim for one major area or a few smaller ones. We cannot sustain change in too many different areas all at once. It takes time, effort, and energy to create new habits. Habits are the regular steps that bring our goal and vision into reality (Clear, 2018).

Take starting a spiritually-based business for example. At the very least it helps to start with a basic plan, including a business and marketing plan. Know your finances, resources and sustainable time commitments. You also need a plan B and to know when to re-evaluate or even when to shut it down. You need to know when it is not working and what is not sustainable. You need to know your own timeline and risk tolerance level.

It is also important to note that the process of making changes can bring up discomfort in itself. This doesn't mean you are doing anything wrong or that your goals are not possible. As we move into the versions of ourselves we want to be, it is common for subconscious and unconscious patterns and beliefs to pop up. It is important to keep committed to your inner work as you take steps towards your goals.

Life purpose can be a tricky concept. It has different meanings for different people. Personally, I don't believe our life purpose is limited to any one area or role we play. I also think we get to have a say in creating a life that is meaningful to us. This can change and evolve over time. It is important to be clear on your top values and priorities and to have a grounded plan for executing your vision. If how this works out in the end changes from your initial vision, know that it is all part of the process. It is not a matter of failure but is a matter of knowing what you need and what is best for you. Our life purpose is not limited to one thing. It is not only connected to our spiritual selves (Miller, 2023) but also something we have to actively engage with and create meaning from in how we live our lives (Frankl, 2006; Kubrick, 2023).

Reflection Questions:

- What stood out to you the most in this section?
- Do you tend to focus more on achieving physical goals or with practicing spiritually based manifestation?
- What do you notice about your own patterns?
- What is working well for you?
- What is not working in the way you would like it to?
- What is the one goal that you most want to manifest?

- What are the SMART goals you can begin to explore to take you into this direction?
  - Specific:
  - Measurable:
  - Attainable:
  - Relevant:
  - Time Bound:
- How can you tell the difference between when it is time to get clear on your current feelings, dreams and desires and when it is time to start taking some type of action?
- What are the steps you can start taking for the universe to meet you there? Think of this like a partnership between you and the universe. In a true partnership, you work together, one side does not carry the full responsibility for both parties in a partnership.
- Do you wait for things to be perfect or want it all figured out before taking a step? (This can keep you stuck).
- What are the slow, steady, and sustainable steps you can take in your current circumstances?

Take steps and be open to signs, synchronicities, opportunities and miracles along the way.

6

Mental Health, Trauma & Spirituality

The realization that we are so much more than our physical bodies alone can be profoundly helpful. A felt experience of connection with something greater than ourselves can increase our resiliency and be a source of comfort and support in challenging times. I am in no way dismissing how helpful and healing this type of connection can be. What I am calling attention to is the issue of ignoring the important role that being in the human body holds in terms of our healing journey. It is not enough to only focus on the spiritual and to ignore the body, mind, and nervous system.

What many popular spiritually-based messages fail to take into account is that even if we are spiritual beings having a human experience, we are still having a human experience! It is still important to understand how to work with and support our physical, human experience. This means that we also have experiences within our brains and nervous systems. It means we come into this existence with a unique set of genetic predispositions and vulnerabilities. Our unique predispositions are shaped by our life experiences, for better or for worse. Our brains and bodies store trauma or experiences of overwhelm in different ways, and so much of this falls outside of our conscious control (Levine, 1997; Van der Kolk, 2015; Winfrey & Perry, 2021).

We also hold a great potential for healing. To help us on our healing path we also need to release the stigma of addressing physical and mental health as a part of our healing journeys. It is not a failure or less spiritual to take medication for your concerns. It is also not always enough to just focus on keeping your thoughts "positive". We often also have to first create a foundation of safety in our nervous systems. We need ways to move through trauma and past negative life experiences. These ways must work with what our bodies, brains, and nervous systems actually need for healing (Levine, 2010; Van der Kolk, 2015; Winfrey & Perry, 2021). I will cover each of these topics in greater detail in this section. I hope that it will help to reduce the stigma around mental health and treatment options.

Stigma Around Mental Health Treatment

The stigma surrounding mental health still exists in our culture (Corrigan & Watson, 2002), and spiritual teachings are not immune to this. This belief can be deeply harmful and is unnecessary. We are multidimensional beings and need to address all aspects of ourselves, our physical bodies, brain, and nervous system health as well as our thoughts and spiritual selves. If our focus is only on "changing our thoughts or vibrations" this can be far too limited to be effective. It can lead to the risk of people feeling like they are "failing" in their spiritual path if they need medical support or interventions.

This stigma often shows up as some version of the belief that it is somehow 'less spiritual" if someone is seeking mental health treatment. In my practice, this tends to come up most often around internalized stigma with taking medication for mental health concerns. If you could benefit from medication as a part of your overall healing path there is absolutely nothing wrong, shameful, or less spiritual in this. Below I have included a list of common questions and concerns I see in my practice around medication. Keep in mind that I cannot provide advice about medications to anyone (I am not a prescriber). The following reflection questions can be a helpful start to bring to your own personal healthcare provider for further discussion and exploration.

Treating the Decision like a One-Time Choice

Try to avoid thinking about medication as an all-or-nothing, one-time, final decision. I encourage my clients to think about trying medication as a part of a journey. A journey you enter into with a trusted prescriber where you are both monitoring any possible positive and negative effects. To be helpful in the long run, the positive impacts should outweigh any potential negative impacts. You should notice an improvement and that it is helpful.

Finding the right medication and the right dosage for you can be a journey that may take time. There can be ups and downs in the process. It is important to have a good working relationship with those who are a part of your care. There should be regular follow-ups to monitor any side effects and progress (often every few weeks for a new medication). You should feel comfortable contacting them to check in if you notice any significant concerns.

There are certain situations where medication is a necessary part of effective treatment. There are also times when it is highly recommended as part of an overall recovery plan. Certain mental health conditions may require medication over the longer term. In general, when concerns are causing moderate to significant symptoms, then a combination of medication and therapy has been generally shown to have the best results (Sammons & McGuinness, 2015).

Fears of Becoming Dependant on Medication

From my experience, this fear can be one of the most common concerns. I understand where this fear is coming from for a lot of people. There is a worry that taking pills is covering the larger issues. And that even if it may help in the short term, there is a fear that this will create a dependency in the long run. Some mental health concerns do require medication management for the longer term, yet this is not always the case.

Some people are more open to trying medication than others. Even if it is a personal preference to not require medication over the long term there are times when medication (as a part of an overall treatment plan) can actually help to achieve wellness the long run. If you have been in therapy and are not seeing the changes you had hoped for, medication can be a helpful combination (American Psychological Association, 2017; Wegmann, 2021). A mentor of mine explained medication this way for treating mental health concerns: it is like if you break your leg and you get a cast to help it heal. No one likes wearing a cast; it can be clunky, annoying, and get in the way. But without the cast, the injury does not heal properly. It creates more complications in the long run. Wearing the cast until the healing is complete is essential to proper healing and living without the cast again.

The key themes I have seen in clients who successfully transition off of taking medication is that if there are situational factors at play, they take steps to address these concerns. Individuals who do the work of addressing the underlying factors that contributed to their symptoms often have greater success in reducing or eliminating their need for medication. A longer term and gradual plan is generally a safer bet (Baldessarini et al, 2010; Moncrieff, 2019; Viguera, 1997), including working at gaining new coping skills and strategies, making changes in their life, and/or addressing any significant underlying trauma.

And in the cases where you need it long term, what is the problem really? If it helps you to live your best life why should it be an issue? We do not shame physical health concerns in the same way there is still stigma attached to mental health concerns and medications. We would not shame someone with diabetes for being "dependent" on insulin for the rest of their lives. This logic would make no sense. The same should be true for mental health medication. If you do need it for the rest of your life but you are living a better life than without it, let's do better and drop the stigma. Always consult with your own health care provider to have a plan for your personal situation (American Psychological Association, 2017).

Concerns that Medication may not Help or that it will Makes Things Worse

Each person's journey with medication is unique. I have seen medication work wonders for people. I have seen people report not much change. I have seen a small minority of people experience scary side effects. No one can know with 100% certainty what your journey with medication may or may not look like. Keep in mind that it tends to be more of a rare event for medication to make things significantly worse. This is why it is important that the decision to consider medication is not an all-or-none choice. Approach the medication journey as an experiment and keep note of the benefits as well as the costs that you notice. It is also important to have an idea of what to anticipate on the journey with your doctor. This can include factors such as how long it should take to start to notice an improvement, possible side effects and so forth. If it feels like symptoms are getting worse, especially if you notice a start or increase in suicidal thoughts, contact your healthcare professional right away (Smith et al., 2020).

Questioning if Symptoms are Really "That Bad" to Need Medication

Perhaps things could get worse, but do you really want that? Like most physical health conditions, efforts toward prevention and early intervention work best. Delaying treatment can make symptoms worse in the long run (Jorm, 2011; Mental Health FirstAid, 2020; Smith & Book 2008). Why wait for concerns to become entrenched patterns? I think the more important question is, could medication be a helpful part of an overall treatment plan? And because most of us tend to be our own toughest critics, it can also be helpful to ask ourselves if a friend or family member was feeling this way, would we judge them for considering medication?

Even if you feel that your situation is currently manageable and you are not interested in exploring medication at this time it can be a helpful exercise to make a list of how you would know when it is time to consider trying medication. What symptoms would be concerning? What intensity? How long?

Knowing the line helps us to know when we have reached it or crossed the threshold.

Worry That Medication Will Change Who you Are

Medication should not change who you are. The hard truth of the matter is that untreated mental health symptoms do have a very real impact on our ability to show up in the world as our authentic selves. You are not your depression/ anxiety/trauma/mental health concern. Treating mental health concerns is about restoring your ability to connect with who you really are. The right medication should help you get back to feeling like yourself, or even help you discover who you have always been underneath the old layers of symptoms or trauma.

Concerns of Diminished Spiritual Connection

Another common concern for intuitive clients is the worry that medication will negatively impact their connection with their intuition or spirituality. This should not be the case when medication is a helpful part of an overall treatment plan. I have not seen this to be the case in my clinical practice. In fact, it is often the opposite. When medication helps it contributes to an improvement in overall quality of life. This includes the ability to more clearly separate the wisdom of intuition from other mental health symptoms. There are also times when medication can be helpful in maintaining a con- nection with reality and with a sense of safety. This may mean helping to "turn off" or "numb" intuition. In some mental health conditions, there may be an overlap of intuition and mental health concerns. There are times when it can be actually helpful to dampen or shut down intuition to focus on the foundations of safety and stability first.

Potential Impact on Health/Life Insurance

In my experience, this one is often the least talked about or considered area of concern. I highlight it here because the potential impact is real and is a matter of concern. It is important to check any health/life insurance policies you may have and their policies around coverage if you do decide to try medication. With some insurance policies, there can be repercussions and your coverage can be impacted when pursuing certain mental health treatments and/or medications. To be clear I strongly do not agree with such policies. I think it creates an unnecessary and discriminatory barrier to accessing treatment. I also don't understand how it makes sense; treating mental health concerns is far better than not. Yet, I also believe in the importance of making a fully informed decision and exploring your options. I would encourage you to do your own research and seek qualified support and guidance to come to the right decision for you. My call to insurance companies is to do better. There should be other options that support a sustainable insurance model and also serve the people whom they are supposed to be helping.

Reflection Questions:

- What stood out the most for me in this section?
- What were the messages about mental health and mental health treatment I was exposed to growing up? In my immediate family? In my larger culture?
- How do I feel about different treatment options for mental health?
- How have my own beliefs about mental health changed and evolved over time?
- How would I know if it might be time to consider/ talk to my health care provider about the potential to explore treatment options for possible mental health concerns?
- Questions that stood out for me to ask my provider if I could benefit from medication include?

Final Reflections on Stigma Around Mental Health

There has been much positive movement towards the destigmatization of mental health compared to a few generations ago (Pescosolido et al. 2021; Paral et al., 2022). There is also still work to be done. At the end of the day, the decision to consider mental health treatment options, including medication, is a personal one and it is up to you who you wish to share this information with. If you notice any of this internalized stigma coming up in yourself I would encourage you to continue to reflect on this.

I hope this section has helped to plant seeds for further reducing the potential for stigma. I also hope it serves to empower you to make choices around your healing team and all treatment options that may be available to you. This section was a very general discussion and is not meant to speak to any one diagnosis or set of symptoms. An individual assessment with a qualified provider is required to provide diagnosis and treatment recommendations.

In the next section, we will cover an overview of the impact of trauma on our nervous systems and how this understanding is important in our approach to our healing journey.

7

The Importance of Understanding the Role of Trauma

We already discussed the issue of ignoring the "human" in "spiritual beings having a human experience" statements. This is a major issue due to the fact that our current nervous system and brain are the result of hundreds of thousands of years of evolution on this planet (to millions of years depending if we are tracing back to modern humans or to common ancestors beyond). (Smithsonian, 2023; Stringer & Andrews, 2011). When we sense danger, whether this danger is real or imagined, our bodies and brains kick into high gear for survival. Our hearts pound faster, muscles tighten, blood pressure rises, breath quickens, pupils dilate, and senses become sharper (McCarty, 2016). This increases our physical strength, stamina, focus, speed, and reaction time - a very adaptive response if you need to run or fight off a wild animal (Harvard Heath Publishing, 2020; Nunez, 2020; Schoen,

2014; Sperber, 2021). This could be in the experience or witnessing of an event that threatens our safety or that of someone we love. It can also be the "death by a thousand cuts" experiences of ongoing threat, lack of safety or support. It is not so much what we experience per say, but what happens within our nervous systems as a result.

However, the downside is that blood flow shifts away from the higher-level thinking part of the brain (prefrontal cortex), and into the emotional brain (limbic system). In response to a threat (real or imagined), we revert back to earlier survival responses. We react to immediate serious or chronic threats by engaging fight, flight, freeze reactions. Our nervous system prioritizes offensive & defensive processes and shuts down healthier ones. This essentially disconnects some parts of the body, emotions, and brain from one another. Trauma is the label given to the original overwhelm and the lingering aftereffects. We often think of post-traumatic stress disorder in association with trauma. Yet we can all carry the impact of unprocessed overwhelm in our nervous systems even without meeting diagnostic criteria for PTSD. Research is now showing that most chronic emotional and physical illnesses have some root source in trauma (Levine & Frederick, 1997; Van der Kolk, 2015, Winfrey & Perry, 2021).

The original traumatic event is like getting hit with a baseball bat. It leaves a sore spot. And when we run into situations that remind us of the original event it is like we have been "poked" in the sore spot again. Our emotional experiences from the past flood or blur into our current experience of reality. This is usually linked to emotions such as fear, anxiety, overwhelm, reactivity, anger, helplessness, shame, and so forth. When our automatic emotional reaction feels out of proportion to the current situation there is likely an aspect of trauma at play. This is not something we can control with conscious thought alone. We need ways to process the impact of old emotional memory or trauma in our nervous systems in order to reduce its impact on us.

Telling a trauma survivor to just "think positively" is incredibly invalidating and misinformed. We cannot just visualize or "positive think"our way out of trauma responses. We need to have tools and ways to work with this automatic response. Ways to help this system to calm and return to a place of safety in order to regain access to our rational and intuitive abilities. We cannot access higher-order states of consciousness from a state of overwhelm.

By the time we are old enough (and ready), to start on our healing journeys we already have most of our early unconscious and subconscious programming in place. We are not all starting from the same place. The tools that can work well for one person will not be what works for everyone. A person who grew up surrounded by safety and love, who had their basic needs met and who experienced attentive, attuned caregivers has a head start. All else being equal, this person is much more likely to be able to self-regulate and respond rather than react. This will give them an advantage in being able to bring their goals into the world. On the flip side, another individual who did not have these basic needs in their early years is going to have a harder time. They will have to put in a lot more effort and energy into just regulating their nervous system and learning to be safe. They will have healing work to do to be able to respond to reality rather than being a victim of the automatic reactions of their nervous systems. "Manifesting"messages will work better for the former individual than they will for the latter. For the trauma survivor, this message also has the potential to do additional harm. They often risk reinforcing shaming and victim/survivor blaming messages. It is important to understand this so that we can all do better in creating a more trauma-informed society.

Signs/Symptoms of Trauma

According to the DSM-V (American Psychological Association, 2017) signs and symptoms of trauma include: involuntary memories that are intrusive and cause distress. Trauma can also show up in the content of our dreams, where dreams are distressing, continue to reoccur and are related to the original trauma. Trauma survivors also experience dissociative reactions and experience intense psychological distress when they are faced with reminders of the original trauma. This distress is automatic and occurs without conscious control. It can often seem to come out of nowhere. We may not even be aware of the link between or what the cue is that connects the original trauma with the flooding of intense distress in the present moment.

This can often lead to ongoing avoidance of reminders of the traumatic event or events, such as attempts to avoid thinking about it, feelings that are related and avoiding external reminders. There are marked changes in ways of thinking and feeling that are a part and parcel of trauma. This includes negative changes in thoughts and mood following a traumatic event or events. There may be an inability to remember parts or all of the traumatic event itself. There can be intrusive and exaggerated changes in autonomic thoughts, such as survivors blaming themselves for what happened. "Negative" emotional states such as anger, fear, horror, guilt and shame can become chronic and pervasive. Trauma survivors often lose interest and may even stop engaging in the things they used to enjoy, such as withdrawing from family and friends and not participating in previous hobbies and self care activities. It is also common to experience feelings of detachment or estrangement from others, like you cannot connect or relate. There is also a persistent inability to feel the most "positive" emotions such as happiness, love and satisfaction.

The nervous system also shows an increase in overall arousal and reactivity. Such as feelings of irritability with little or no provocation, reckless or self-destructive behaviour, hypervigilance, exaggerated startle response, problems with concentration and sleep disturbances. All of these symbols combined results in a significant decline and negative impact in important areas of life, such as overall well-being, relationships, self-care, career and more.

How Trauma Can Show Up

Some of the ways that unprocessed trauma can show up can include feeling stuck or unable to break free from repeating patterns. No matter how much awareness you have, when similar triggers come up you go right back into previous patterns. This is often best described as reacting in the moment rather than responding. It feels like you have little to no conscious control over your knee-jerk reactions in the face of similar triggers. The emotional energy in these times is intense. The emotions feel intense, overwhelming and unpleasant. Often fear, anger, panic, distress, wanting to run away, rage, or shut down. Your fight, flight or freeze response is activated. Your reactions often don't make sense in their intensity in the present day. Another tricky thing about unprocessed trauma symptoms is that they often get worse with age or at a certain phase of life. This can be because there may be more emotional, physical, mental, spiritual supports and resources and overall feelings of safety at later stages of life, to be able to process the trauma. Often this seems counterintuitive and does not make sense to people at the time. It can also come up at similar life stages. An example is childhood trauma becoming activated as a parent when a child reaches the same age/stage as when the original trauma occurred. When this occurs the emotional experience is intense and the person who is having the experience may or may not be consciously aware of where these intense emotions are rooted in the past rather than the present.

What People Often Report

A range of intense and difficult emotions are often common with unprocessed trauma, feelings of frustration (feeling frustrated with themselves, with the situations, with others) and anxiety, fear, and avoidance of similar events or triggers. This is often due to the fact that things can feel just fine, as long as we avoid the reminders that bring up intense, unpleasant emotions. Depending on the nature of the trauma this can really limit our potential and our lives. A fear of snakes? Probably not a big deal in our day-to-day lives, as, in most of our lives we have control over how much we are around snakes. Fear of intimacy and getting close to others? Fear of success? Fear of hard conversations? Any other area that can have a major impact on life and relations? You get the idea, that the impact can be significant when these triggers are left unaddressed. The cost of avoiding connection and growth is a huge price to pay in major areas of our lives and happiness.

I am a strong believer in the healing potential of trauma-healing and trauma-based information. Without this education people often feel like they are not trying hard enough or feel like a failure. It feels like change is impossible or very, very difficult. This is because addressing trauma needs to be rooted in an understanding of how trauma impacts our bodies, brains, and nervous systems. Without this understanding, the risk is high that people can internalize a sense of failure. This can add to feelings of hopelessness and have a negative impact on their sense of self-esteem and personal agency.

The Good News

The good news is that healing is also possible. It is often about finding the right approaches and tools for you as an individual. It may also involve finding the right and safe support. Healing the past does not mean that we forget or lose the memory of what happened. It means we move closer and closer to freedom from the overwhelming emotions of the past in the present. When trauma symptoms get more intense and distressing, this can be a sign that our bodies and minds are ready to begin to release and heal. The key is finding the right approaches and support and moving forward in a safe way. Trauma symptoms do not have to be a life sentence. We cannot always control what has happened to us but we do get a choice of how to move forward from where we are now. Trauma was not our fault and yet healing is our opportunity and responsibility, individually and as a collection.

Keys to Healing and Integration

Some of the first steps on the road to trauma healing are to find ways to help you come back to a feeling of safety in the present moment. This is often referred to as grounding and containment strategies. We need a strong foundation of safety and a sense of control in the present before diving too deeply. If we move too quickly we risk moving into over-whelm, which can be more harmful than helpful. These tools give us a way to come out and back into the present moment. Many trauma processing modalities include techniques to help maintain nervous system regulation. Once grounded in the moment then it is safe to bring up the old emotions and physical sessions. This helps the brain process the old raw emotions and sensations, so that they can have less impact on the present day. The key is to be able to stay out of going into an automatic fight-flight or freeze reaction. This can result in re-traumatization rather than healing. No one technique works for everyone, it is about finding the right approach for each individual. If working on your own is overwhelming, seek professional support. Look for a professional with training and experience in trauma processing. Finding a good fit and someone you can build trust with is essential.

Post-Traumatic Growth

It is also important to talk about post-traumatic growth in the wake of a difficult experience. Post-traumatic growth is the positive change that occurs as a result of exposure to adversity and challenge. It is not a direct result of the trauma itself. (And is not something that should be used to bypass the real harm caused by trauma). But it is any of the positive outcomes that come from difficult times from how you cope in the face of adversity. 30 - 70% of individuals who have faced adversity also report positive growth coming out of the experience (Colliner, 2016; Tedeschi & Calhoun, 1996).

Post-Traumatic Growth Tends to Occur in Five Areas

1) A sense that new opportunities/possibilities have emerged from the challenge.

2) Positive changes in relationships with others (increased connection/closeness).

3) Increased Sense of one's own strength.

4) Greater appreciation for life in general.

5) Deeper spiritual/religious growth or change in belief system.

Reflection Questions:

- Where might my own self-sabotage patterns be rooted in my nervous system rather than in my conscious mind?
- How can I practice more compassion for myself and others?
- Do I suspect or know that I have a history of unprocessed past trauma?
- If so, how can I have more compassion for myself and my symptoms?
- What tools and practices do I have to help me work with and support my nervous system in moving through or out of a fight-flight-freeze response?
- What resources and support are available to help me?

- Even if I do not have my own unprocessed trauma, how can I be more sensitive to the experiences of others who are still struggling with the aftermath of trauma in their brains and bodies?
- How have I grown from how I coped with difficult times?

No matter where you are starting from, the good news is that we can all make progress from where we are. We are also capable of healing in the right conditions and support. Small steps over time can make a major impact when we look at longer time frames.There are more and more tools and supports out there to help us on our journey. We cannot ignore the impact of the brain and nervous system on our healing paths. There is great potential for healing in combining the wisdom and tools from multiple practices and perspectives in order to address all levels of our being.

A Spiritual Awakening Itself can be Traumatic

A spiritual awakening itself can be a traumatic experience under certain conditions. As we previously discussed, increasing spiritual connection ideally needs to be done in a safe and gradual way. If there are concerns with significant mental health symptoms the focus should be on stability first. Before pushing for further intuitive opening. The aim should be for healing and integration along the journey. The path looks different for each individual (Corneille & Luke, 2021). An awakening can feel intense at times but it does not have to be traumatic and a traumatic awakening can do more harm than good. I am not in favour of increasing intuitive or spiritual awakening when someone is significantly struggling or in a state of crisis. This can look different from person to person depending on their situation.

In addition, if someone has a history of unprocessed trauma then a spiritual awakening can have the potential to be traumatic itself. Moving too quickly into spiritual experiences can bring up symptoms in a way that is destabilizing rather than helpful. There needs to be enough safety and integration to hold the new, expanded states of consciousness. Without a stable enough container an awakening can lead to a breakdown rather than expansion. This can even result in post traumatic stress disorder symptoms for some individuals.

I cannot stress enough the importance of having safe and knowledgeable support along this path. There can be higher risks with self-proclaimed healers or facilitators who do not have culturally appropriate training or experience. As well as with anyone who is not sufficiently trauma-trained or informed. Practices that accelerate awakening experiences, (including but not limited to psychedelics) can be another risky area. Especially when used outside of appropriate context and support. And when there is limited or no screening, preparation, and integration. In traditional cultures people were given support and time away to help make sense of and to integrate these experiences. In these societies people do much better than they do in more Western medical model based cultures such as our own (Borges & Tomlinson, 2016).

The goal is not to open as quickly as possible. This can be problematic or even dangerous. It is so important to have a foundation of safety before any practices that may 'open up' your awareness or have the potential to go too deep, too quickly. Aim to remain grounded and stable as you explore your awakening. To be able to integrate your spiritual reality and experiences in your day-to-day world.

Reflection Questions:

- Do I have a history of trauma that has not been addressed or processed?
- What support do I have in place or access to if exploring my spiritual awakening or intuitive connection becomes too intense or does not feel safe?
- If I am interested in exploring processes that claim to accelerate spiritual openings, do the teachers and or also understand these concerns? Is there a screening process to assess for safety and stability in these programs or experiences?
- Do any programs or work I am considering screen for unprocessed trauma, screen for or include grounding and stability as well as practices that facilitate openings?
- What type of support (if any) is available in case

someone is not feeling safe or if and awakening is becoming destabilizing?

- If I am considering a retreat or the use of traditional cultural practices or medicines what is the training path the practitioners or facilitators have taken? What is their mental health training or what resources are available? Do they seem to understand the risks? Do they seem to be aware of the risks that processes that accelerate spiritual opening may not be safe or recommended for everyone at all times?

If you have current mental health symptoms or a history of unprocessed trauma, please proceed carefully with spiritual practices. Spiritual practices can be a helpful part of a recovery path but too much too soon can end up doing more harm than good. It is very important to find safe and knowledge support as you proceed on your own path. Proceed with caution and seek professional support or consultation for your own situation.

8

Red Flags in Spiritual Healers and Teachers

When I was looking for support in navigating my own spiritual awakening I didn't know what I didn't know. I had little to no awareness of what the red or green flags were. From my clinical work and experience, I know I am not alone in this. There have been so many times I have validated clients' experience of "how could they have known". After all, it is not like there is a credible guidebook out there. This is a big part of my why for creating this guidebook!

It can be very helpful to have safe and trusted practitioners and guides on our spiritual path. The concern is that not everyone is helpful or even safe. I have seen major harm result from negative experiences with once-trusted healers or teachers. I have also had my own negative experiences with those I had once trusted in this space. Trusting the wrong people can do more harm than good. I have also been fortunate to have some amazing teachers and guides. My hope is to help empower you to find the people and spaces that will be healing and helpful. And to know what to look out for to avoid those who are not (Rankin, 2022, 2022). It is worth taking the time to find the right support.

Differences in Regulated and Unregulated Spaces

It is often difficult to know who can help or where to turn to. This may lead to a search for help in regulated as well as unregulated spaces. Before we dive in deeper I wanted to quickly summarize some of the key differences in each space.

Regulated professionals include protected titles where there is a minimum standard of training and competency (Alberta Government, 2024). Titles such as: Psychiatrist, Doctor, Registered Psychologist, Registered Social Worker, Registered Massage Therapist, Naturopathic Doctor, etc. All regulated professionals have a code of ethics and a regulatory body that they are accountable to. There are often rigorous standards of training and supervision in order to become a member. They have guidelines and rules that are designed to protect the public. However, this is not perfect in terms of meaning that there are never violations or breaches. There is a clear standard of care and ethical guidelines. There are also clear steps to investigation and to disciplinary action from these bodies for anyone who is a member. Registered professionals are also often required to hold practice insurance. This means that if there is harm caused by their actions there is insurance in place to pay damages.

When we get into the unregulated spaces there is less of this built-in safety, training, and accountability. Unprotected titles can include unregulated titles such as: healer, counsellor, coach, energy worker, spiritual healer, and so forth. This means that training and experience can vary wildly. It also means there is no outside body to bring serious concerns to. If you do suffer harm you may be limited to deciding whether to pursue legal or civil action on your own. There is often no requirement that the practitioner will hold liability insurance. This may reduce the likelihood of you receiving any award damages if they are unable to pay.

I am in no way saying or suggesting that all alternative or spiritual teachers/healers or community leaders are harmful or dangerous. On the flip side, I am also not claiming that all members of regulated health professionals are immune to causing harm. There is a small minority in any profession who cause harm to those whom they are meant to be helping. The key point is that a greater degree of due diligence and research is often warranted in unregulated spaces. This is because there are fewer checks and balances built in place to ensure public safety.

The God Complex

The God complex is a red flag to be aware of. If anyone is claiming to be almost superhuman I would be highly doubtful of their credibility. This can show up in a few different areas such as claiming to have all the answers, be fully healed, or insistence that their way is the only valid path. And once you know where to look you will likely notice more examples. The following information is to help you peek behind the curtain and see through these tactics.

Those who Claim to Have all the Answers

I would advise proceeding with caution with anyone who claims to have all the answers. We can each have expertise in a few select areas but not one of us knows everything or what is best for everyone. It is impossible to be an expert on everything. I would be hesitant to trust anyone who behaves as if they have the authority to speak on every subject, especially without evidence of the sources of their deeper knowledge and understanding. At the very least they should be able to acknowledge their frame of reference. If they do neither of these things, be very cautious. This may be someone who just likes to hear themselves speak and is feeding a shadow side of their own ego.

At the very least someone should be sharing what their teachings are based on. Wherever the source, is it coming from a "channeled message", their own experience, a collection of case studies, or up-to-date research findings? Speaking on topics as if it is undisputed "fact" without a clear grounding in where the information coming from is a red flag. At the very least you should be empowered to do your own research and make your own informed choices.

Possible Warning Signs can Include:

- They claim to serve anyone and everyone.
- They do not seem to offer guidance on who they can best support (and who is better supported elsewhere).
- They do not recognize the limits to their own knowledge base.
- They can come off as confident, yet their teachings are not accurate or informed by real-world data.
- They do not allow their "authority" to be questioned.

There is so much information available to us in this digital and information age. The challenge is to be able to sort through it all to see what is helpful and what is just another opinion. I have heard some so-called spiritual teachers (some with large audiences) spout off a bunch of complete nonsense. Without any indication that they even realize that they do not know what they are talking about. Look for someone who has the experience and credibility you need for what you are looking for. No one has all the answers and those who think they do may end up not being the best option to support you on your path.

Anyone Claiming to be "Fully Healed"

I am not saying that being "fully healed" isn't possible. Only that I have not seen it. It is also not something I personally strive for or would encourage others to strive for. Findings from quantum physics show that the very nature of our reality is change and flow. That energy is always evolving, expanding, flowing (McTaggart, 2008; Talbot, 2011). If this is the natural state of existing how could we ever expect that we will ever fully "arrive"?

If someone is presenting themselves as beyond the human condition I would proceed very cautiously. This in itself can be a huge red flag. The chances are high that they are not in a place of integrity in their work, or how their own unhealed shadow stuff can be highly problematic. I have far more trust for the teachers and guides who acknowledge being human and not being perfect. Those who focus on the process and tools to bring themselves back into acting from their values. Emphasizing the practice of returning to a regulated, loving, compassionate space over and over again. Rather than trying to teach that any human should only ever be there.

I would also be very cautious with anyone who claims to be superior to others or claims to have almost "god-like" abilities. Could it be possible? Perhaps. Are most people there? Probably not. And if our interaction with someone is new and on a more surface level then we will not be able to see what might lurk beneath the surface at first glance. It takes time and experience to get to know someone's true character.

Like with any new relationship, take time and don't rush in. Trust needs to be earned over time. A true healer or guide who is doing their work will not be turned off by this. They will support what you need to feel safe and they will understand that trust needs to be built over time.

Promoting Their Way as the Only Way

I would also advise caution with anyone who insists that their path is the only valid way. Healers and guides, like friends, may come into your life for a reason, a season, or a lifetime. We don't usually know at the start what your path with one person is possible to be. What learnings will unfold together? No one person outside of yourself holds the key to your healing and transformation.

There are many possible helpful and valid pathways to healing. It is about finding the approaches that work best for you in each season of your journey. It is not about finding the way. It is about finding your own way. Helpful healers and guides will aim to help empower you to connect with your own path.

Mistaking Spiritual Abilities for Integrity

This is a big one that I wish I had known earlier on and that I have seen many people get tripped up on. Someone can be very gifted psychically but this does not mean they should automatically be trusted to have your best interests at heart.

It is easy to fall into the trap of confusing psychic or intuitive ability with trustworthiness and integrity. Intuitive ability is not a reflection of integrity or safety on its own. I would not advise looking for someone who seems to be the most psychically gifted. This in itself is not enough to make an informed decision about if they are the right support. Look for someone who you feel safe with, who you see is walking their talk and acting from a place of integrity. Who also understands the spiritual realms and seems like they could help you with your goals.

A teacher or healer may be a longer-term relationship but you should also be evolving and active within your own healing work as a part of the process. Intuitive ability is similar to any other skill set. Some people come into this world with a stronger connection and ability. It comes more easily and naturally to them. Just like some individuals are more athletically gifted, academically inclined, musically talented, and so forth. All of us can still develop and improve our skills with time, practice, and perseverance.

For now, it is enough to know that intuitive or psychic skill on its own it is not enough to tell if someone will be safe to work with. Psychic ability alone is not a sign of integrity or trustworthiness on its own. Spiritual gifts in the wrong hands can end up doing a lot more damage than good. Try to hold yourself back from putting anyone on a pedestal. Keeping this in mind can save you a lot of potential trouble.

Always check in with your own intuition and be clear on your core values and how you can know when someone is acting from a place of integrity or not. We will cover green flags in more depth in the next chapter.

Promoting Dependency over Personal Empowerment

Some of the most common ways that a so-called spiritual healer or teacher can promote dependency include: by trying to be the source of your answers for you, claiming to know your future, and using scare tactics. I will break down each of these red flags in further detail below.

Being the Source of Your Answers

It has been my experience that we all have our own source of knowing within ourselves (our intuition). A part of stepping into our own power is not giving away the authority for our own lives to anyone outside of ourselves. A skilled teacher can be a helpful guide on the path but they should not be walking the path for you. They can point the way but you should still hold responsibility for your decisions and ultimately your life. Intuitive information is filtered through our own lenses and interpretations too. It is not an exact science. Even the most skilled intuitive practitioner can get things wrong.

Anyone who is trying to create a dependence on them

instead of helping to empower you is cause for concern. This is basically a spiritual version of someone fishing for you instead of teaching you to fish. That is not to say that there cannot be a lot of value in having trusted support to go to for guidance. Yet, no one outside of yourself should hold the ultimate responsibility for the choices that are for you to make in your own life. After all, for better or for worse, it is your life. We are each responsible for and accountable for the choices we make in our own lives. Learning to "fish" for yourself can be a longer and more active process on your part than relying on someone else to give you the answers or messages. Yet it is an investment in developing this part of yourself. A connection that can continue to evolve and be of service to you over your lifetime. Would you rather have to keep going outside of yourself or be able to turn to your own inner knowing anytime?

Don't be surprised if you have been stuck in this pattern and you end up receiving bad advice or a clearly "wrong" intuitive reading. This is also something that can show up for people as a sign to stop going outside of yourself for answers. It may be time to reflect if you are ready to commit to the practice of developing your own connection with your intuition. Relationships, including those with healers and guides, can come into our lives 'for a reason, season or a lifetime'. When a relationship has run its course it may be meant to break down to make space for a new way of relating.

Developing intuitive ability can be a process that takes

time and working with the right teachers and guides can be highly valuable. Some skills are worth investing in. Only you can know/decide if this is a connection you want to build for yourself. And if it is, find those who will support you in developing your own connection with this part of yourself. A healer who is in their integrity should not want to be a substitute for your own intuition and discernment.

Signs You may be Looking for Answers Outside of Yourself

- Going to someone for quick answers without committing to making changes yourself.
- Going to multiple practitioners to get the answer(s) you want to hear.
- Only going to someone when you are in a state of panic or crisis. Not remaining committed to doing your own work outside of these times.

These flags may be a sign that you may be approaching a teaching/healing relationship from a place of wanting someone to give you answers or do the work for you. Only you can decide if this is helping you in the long run or if it is contributing to keeping you stuck.

Claiming Your Future is Set in Stone

I have seen clients become stressed out (or even devastated) by some of the messages they have received from an intuitive reader or healer. These messages often share a common theme of predicting only one possible outcome in an area of life. A proclamation that the client will never have what they desire in this lifetime. Messages such as you will never have a happy relationship, you are here to struggle/suffer, you will not be able to get what you want (children, career, life goals, etc). It is not someone's place to tell you what is or is not possible for you or that there is only one outcome to these types of questions.

Anyone who claims to know your entire future is not someone to trust or place your faith in. There is much we cannot control but we also have free will and many areas of influence. There are many things we cannot control in this life. There may be karmic and soul-level forces at play. Yet it is also true that on a quantum level, there are infinite realities out there. Be wary of anyone who claims that there is only one possible outcome available to you in any area of your life. For example, if we want children we can explore any and all avenues available to us. We can be open to having a family through means other than birthing our own children. If we desire a loving romantic partnership we can remain commit-ted to our own healing work. We can learn about healthy communication and healthy relationship patterns. We can date more intentionally while still living our best lives in the moment. Even if we have not had healthy partnerships, there are steps we can take to change this. It is not set in stone.

You should not give up on what you desire because someone outside of yourself tells you that it is not possible for you. It is not for anyone outside of ourselves to tell us how our lives will play out. We get a say. What we do in each moment matters. We are active creators of our own futures. There are multiple futures available to all of us at any given time. Yes, there are things in life that are beyond our control. But no one outside of ourselves should be telling us when it is time to grieve the death of a dream. There is a difference when we allow ourselves to go through our own process and come to our own decisions. Things will not always turn out the way we may have initially wanted but so much more can come our way.

Trust in your own process and your own intuition and logic. And if you have ever had a "bad" reading write it out, rip it up, and burn it, let that sucker go. Harness your feelings about it to take steps towards what you do want. Never let someone outside of yourself tell you what you are or are not capable of.

Using Scare Tactics

Healing work is a sacred space and needs to be treated as such. At the very least, there should be a foundation of trust and safety with anyone who you decide to work with. Entering into a healing or mentorship type of relationship is not a decision that should be based on fear.

There is a difference between taking something seriously and the use of scare tactics. A serious concern can be communicated with an energy of *"I really think it is in your best interest to take this seriously/get support with this"*. This recommendation should make sense and feel valid to you. The person communicating this should also not be overly attached if you choose to work with them or someone else. They should encourage you to work with someone who also has the skills, integrity, and experience. It should not feel like it can only be them, as long as you get the support you need.

If someone is trying to use fear to scare you into committing to work with them this is a major red flag. Fear is never the answer or the space to make this type of decision. If it feels like someone is using fear to scare you into working with them- please don't. Walk away, think it over, and ask around for other recommendations.

Reflection Questions:

- Is this practitioner/teacher/leader "walking their talk"?
- Do they position themselves as superior to others?
- Do I have enough experience with them to have established a foundation of real trust?
- What docs my gut and intuition say?
- Do they seem to genuinely want what is best for other's or do they seem more concerned with keeping people

working with them? This may be as a client, mentee, student, etc.?

- Do they get upset, angry or use fear, guilt or shame to keep someone working with them?
- Do they claim to know better than you when it comes to decisions in your own life?
- When I take an outside observer view would I be okay with how this person communicates and with how they conduct themselves?
- Would I trust this person with my friends, loved ones, my children?
- If someone else treated a loved one, friend or my child in the way this person behaves would I be concerned?

Spiritual Abilities in the Hands of Dangerous and Manipulative Personalities

There are many well-meaning people out there. The majority of people fall into this category. I do believe that most people are good and are doing their best. Not all harm is intentional or malicious. Often harm comes from wounded people who end up hurting people. From not knowing better and therefore not being able to do better at a given time. However, there is also a small percentage of people whose behaviour is downright dangerous. Some individuals exhibit low empathy and a high potential for exploitation and manipulation of others. There are some people whose actions and behaviour are harmful and can lead to real trauma in the lives of people who get too close to them

It is important to realize that a small percentage of the population exhibits chronic, persistent and ongoing behaviour that are highly concerning and even dangerous. There are individuals who exhibit high antisocial traits or even antisocial personality disorder. This presents as a failure to conform to social norms, deceitfulness, impulsivity, irritability, aggressiveness, reckless disregard for safety of self or others, consistent irresponsibility, lack or remorse. As well as a pattern of disregard for and violation of the rights of others. There are also those who have high traits of narcissistic personality disorder. This presents as interpersonally exploitative behaviour. Including taking advantage of others, a lack of empathy, and a strong sense of entitlement (American Psychological Association, 2017; Patrick, 2022). It is important to know that spiritually-based communities are not immune to these concerns or personality types (Hassan, 2015). I have seen some of the greatest harm in spiritual spaces come from individuals who are high in harmful personality traits. Especially when they are in a position of power or authority (such as a trusted healer, guide, teacher, etc). They are out there. I have personally encountered people like this. Some have a large or even international public following. Just because someone seems to have a large following does not automatically mean they should be trusted.

For those of us who are more trusting and open by nature,

we need to be aware that there are times when we need to be careful. We need to be mindful to not trust others before they have earned the right to our trust over time and through consistency in their behaviour. Take your time in getting to know someone. Trust is not just about what people preach but about how well their actions line up with their words. Do not give your full trust to someone whom you do not know until you have had time to see their behaviour over time. With a healthy person, this will not damage your relationship. It will help you to keep yourself safe and give you enough time and experience to get a better sense of someone's true colours.

Keep in mind that many dangerous personality types can be very charming and charismatic at first. They are often well-liked and well-respected in public but they show a very different side to those who get close to them. This is when the mask comes off. They are often more concerned with their perceived outside image than how they make the people closest to them feel. They are often well-liked and respected publicly but can be a significant cause of trauma to those they are closest to (American Psychological Association, 2017; Lyons, 2019).

Getting into psychopathy and personality disorders is beyond the scope of this book. I will provide a brief overview to help you to make your own informed decisions and to keep yourself safe in your own journey. My hope is that it can help to just know that people like this exist and are out in the world in general as well as in spiritual communities. It is a small percentage of the population and of course, on a soul level, they are just as worthy as everyone else. Yet your own safety comes first. To be educated is to be prepared. If you suspect you may be dealing with someone with a high degree of these traits please seek your own individual support and guidance.

To be clear, I am not saying that any one diagnosis is a red flag in itself. It depends on the level of self-awareness, accountability, and work that a person is actively doing in order to manage these tendencies. It is not to say that even harmful people cannot change. If someone is willing to look at their own behaviour and to do the work the majority of people can grow. It is only to say that not everyone we encounter will be willing to do the work. And when they are not, it is not your job to try to control what they do or do not do. You need to keep yourself safe first and foremost. Your own healthy boundaries will serve you well here.

Reflection Questions:

- Can the person you are concerned about have a difficult conversation and take accountability in a healthy and mature way? Without becoming defensive, abusive, or shutting you out completely?
- Do you feel like you are dealing with two totally different people? Initially, kind and caring and even charismatic, and then something switches when you get closer and they get comfortable? (The mask slips).

- Does the person you are concerned about seem to have a history of drama and chaos that follows them?
- Do they engage in gaslighting, blame-shifting and DARVO (Deny, Accuse, Reverse Victim, and Offender)? When you try to talk to them about harmful behaviour of theirs they quickly become defensive and shift the blame. They try to make it your fault or put the blame somewhere else to justify their actions.
- Are they able and willing to self-reflect, to apologize, to take appropriate steps to repair ruptures in relationships?
- Are they able to take appropriate accountability? Or do they expect someone to just move on without any repair efforts on their part? Do they get angry or cold if you ask for repair efforts for the harm they have caused?
- Can they continue to hold multiple perspectives, especially during difficult conversations?
- Can they continue to demonstrate empathy for others over time? Especially when someone disagrees with them or brings up a concern with their behaviour. Can they maintain self-regulation and are they able to self-reflect and put themselves in another's shoes?
- Do they seem to have double standards? The rules they expect of others don't seem to apply to them?
- Are the above patterns persistent, chronic, and across multiple situations and relationships?

It is important to note that these traits exist on a spectrum. We can expect parts of these traits at times. The more extreme, persistent, and pervasive these traits are, the more potential harm there is. Especially when the person is not taking steps to manage these traits within themselves. Someone with a history of harmful behaviours should be well into their own longer-term work and management of these patterns before engaging in a healer or teacher role. There is too much potential for harm to potential clients or students otherwise. Unhealthy/unprofessional boundaries often go hand in hand with dangerous personality types. This can include exploitation for personal gain, abusive behaviour, weaponizing spiritual teachings, avoiding accountability and more. I will cover more about healthy boundaries and green flags in the next section to help you to be able to recognize the differences.

9

Green Flags: Finding Safe, Trustworthy, and Ethical Supports

Another area to be aware of in your awakening journey is the role of healthy boundaries. They are an important area in all of our healing journeys. Boundaries include our sense of self, where we end and where another begins. A sense of healthy boundaries helps to protect us and also protect our relationships. They help us to know what is ours to communicate and control and what is not ours. There are often many common unhelpful or even harmful messages related to boundaries in some spiritual spaces. We reviewed common red flags in the previous section. Healthy boundaries protect the client/student as well as the practitioner/teacher. I will cover some of the key areas to be aware of for healthy and professional boundaries. The following section is meant to help serve as a guide for any more formal client/practitioner or student/teacher type of relationship (Psychologists Association of Alberta, 2006) . In less formal settings or situations all of the following may not apply or fit. Knowing the red flags helps us to look out for what we want to avoid. Yet we also need to know the green flags so we can recognize what we are looking for when we find it.

Healthy Boundaries

Clear and Appropriate Boundaries

It is not a reg flag (and likely more a green flag) for a helper, healer, or professional to have appropriate boundaries in their work. In fact, not having the following in place can be a warning sign for possible inappropriate or unprofessional boundaries. These include informed consent, communication, time, scope of practice, and financial boundaries. The following information can help you make an informed decision.

Informed Consent and Practice Policies

If you are entering into any kind of formal agreement there should be clear expectations about what to expect in your work together. This includes what you and what the provider/helper/teacher are responsible for. This is often covered before you even begin to work with the person. This might also include a course outline or expectations for a training or mentorship program. It is important to be able to make an informed decision about what the practitioner/teacher can provide and what is your responsibility. This also includes expectations for termination of services on both sides. Are there any refunds? Can you withdraw consent/terminate services at any time? Are there any consequences if you do? What (if any) are the notice periods to avoid consequences? On what ground would a teacher/practitioner no longer work with a client/student? (Number of no shows/late cancellations, violating behaviour expectations, if the work falls outside of their area of expertise?). This should be discussed before entering into a working relationship together. As well as on an ongoing basis (when appropriate).

Communication Boundaries/Expectations

Expectations and boundaries around communication can include things such as the following. Is there support between scheduled times/sessions? What is appropriate to communicate between scheduled times? How to contact them (by phone, email, text, DMs)? If the information is of a sensitive or personal nature what steps should be taken to ensure confidentiality. This can include limiting communication to secure methods only. Will they be reading or responding to messages sent or will you receive them together at your next scheduled time? If they do respond between appointments, do they bill for this time and how is this broken down? If additional support is needed, what resources are available? One person should not ever be the only option in cases of high risk or crisis. This can be a dangerous situation for the person who is in crisis as one person can not be available 24/7. Clarity on these expectations helps to ensure that you are both on the same page. This way you can make your own informed choice about what will best meet your needs.

Time Boundaries

There can be a version of the belief that a true "helper" is always available/always able to give. This is quite simply not true and is in fact a recipe for burnout. People can and do really want to help and to make a difference and are also not required to be on call 24/7. Burnout is a real risk and an occupational hazard in helping professionals. Healthy time boundaries help practitioners and teachers ensure that they can remain in this work in the long term.

Time boundaries include the following. Expectations around working hours. Such as when are their session/teaching times. When are they available? How soon or when to expect a response? When are they checking messages and how or when do they follow up? What are the expectations around arranging time together? Do you need to book in advance? How far? If you need something and you have not scheduled can they get you in or do they provide referral options? In the majority of cases helping professionals get into the field because they do care about people and want to do work that makes a difference. Yet we are also people too. The work needs to be sustainable over the long term. Keep in mind that a practitioner often has many clients throughout their careers. This can be a hundred to thousands over time. Their policies are there to protect the sustainability of their work. Even if it feels like a quick ask on a client's end, little requests can add up to an unmanageable load fast.

If you are finding you need more support than one person can provide there is nothing wrong or shameful in this in any way. It may just be a sign that a higher level of intervention and support would be more helpful. This may be a sign to move into a more intensive type of support or resources or to increase the number of resources and supports that you are accessing. It is normal for us all to have needs. And we are all worthy and deserving of receiving support. Yet as adults, no one person outside of us can be responsible for meeting all of our needs all of the time. I also acknowledge that there is a lot of work that needs to be done on a social level in terms of increasing access to resources for all.

Boundaries in their Scope of Practice

It is also a green flag for a practitioner or teacher to have boundaries regarding who they work with and what types of clients they can best support. This can be a green flag that they know the limits of their own knowledge and experience and who they can best support. It is also a sign that they are aware of and taking responsibility for their own boundaries. This can also include issues such as capacity boundaries, such as when or if they have openings for new clients. This is where someone cannot provide what you need or is not the best fit (even if you might want them to be) . It is not rejection but redirection. It is a good sign if a practitioner does not take everyone. Ideally, they may be able to direct you to who or where might be a better fit.

Financial Boundaries: Sustainability & Accessibility for Both Practitioners and Clients

There can be a lot of mixed messages around money and finances within popular spiritual teaching. On one extreme there are messages implying that someone is not a "true" healer if they require payment for their time and work. That if someone really wanted to help others, they would be working for free. On the other end of the spectrum is that only those with the highest rates are 'worth' working with. Both extremes can be problematic for their own reasons.

The first belief is that if someone "really" wanted to help they would work for free or on a donation basis is a problem for a number of reasons. Healers need to charge adequately for their services in order for them to suitably continue to be of service. Most practitioners cannot afford to devote themselves to their work without financial compensation. We need to reexamine the expectation that if you want to help people money should not come into play in any way. There are very, very few helpers who get into the field for the money. On a purely logical level alone this path would not make sense in the majority of cases if financial motivation was the only motivation. This track would be a poor investment if the financial reward was your main motivator and goal. There are many other ways to make money (and easier ways to do so if making money was someone's only motivation)! Most helping professionals want to do work they are passionate about, want to be of service but also need to be able to make a living.

A monetary investment often reflects a level of energetic investment, (for those who are fortunate enough to have a level of disposable income). With healing and personal development work the people who get the most out of it are actively involved and motivated in their own process. It is not like going to the dentist where you get shiny clean or new teeth no matter how invested you are in the process. As long as you show up and keep your butt in the chair the end results will be the same. Personal development work is more like personal training. You need to be doing the work as a part of your lifestyle. When people don't value the work and the process there is often a lot of wasted time and energy for all involved. It can be helpful to have some skin in the game in terms of investment. On the flip side again this does not mean going beyond what you can afford.

There can be the opposite belief, that only those who charge the most can help you or be of service. This is also an unhelpful belief. There are many people who can be helpful within all budget ranges. It is not only those who charge the most who can be the most helpful to you. The price point is not always a direct reflection of the level of skill, experience or ability to help. If working with someone is going to put you in a highly stressful financial situation please pause and reflect if this is truly the best or only option. Especially in unregulated spaces, there are a lot of high-pressure sales tactics in coaching and other areas. You do not need thousands of dollars to move towards meaningful change. Many free and low-cost agencies have very skilled professionals who can be of great service if you are willing and able to give it a chance. (I have worked in many of these settings myself, at times overlapping with my work in private practice).

Professional Boundaries

Your healing work and session time should be focused on supporting you in your goals and concerns. There can be a difference between regulated and unregulated professionals here. There should be a clear separation between a professional relationship from a personal one. It is not your job to provide emotional or other support to your practitioners. (It is their job to have appropriate support in place to keep their client's work clean). Your session time should be focused on you and your goals, not a place for your practitioner to talk about their personal life. Physical and sexual boundaries should also always be respected without question. If a practitioner/teacher makes sexual advances on their clients/students, this is automatically a huge reg flag. It is a reportable offences to their regulatory body and it can also be possible to take legal action.

Reflection Questions:

- Does this feel like an unprofessional boundary or is it bringing something else up?
- What has my experience with healthy boundaries been like so far in my life?
- What is something that I used to think was mean or unkind that I now see as a clear, assertive boundary and not an indication that the person does not care about me or the relationship
- What are my own goals for my relationship with my personal boundaries and communication?
- Are there any of these boundaries that I struggle more with holding myself?
- Are there any of these boundaries that I have a harder time being on the recovering end of?

The Need for Systemic Change

I want to make it clear that this section is only for those who are fortunate enough to have some level of discretionary disposable income. There are many people living below the poverty line, who are struggling to secure basic resources such as food, safe housing, medication, reliable transportation, and so on. The following is not meant to apply to anyone in this situation. The role that systemic issues play here cannot be overlooked or discounted. It is very hard or even almost impossible to have the safety and space to focus on healing your past if you are forced to live in survival mode in your day to day. Access to basic needs is foundational in terms of survival and safety. You can't tell someone who is living in a war zone or abusive situation or otherwise just struggling to survive day to day to just "visualize'"how they want to feel to create a better reality. This is not enough on its own. You need safe, resources and basic needs first and foremost.

I also want to be clear that I am a believer and supporter of services being accessible for all, regardless of income. I believe that help should be accessible to anyone who needs it and is motivated to do the work. As individual practitioners, we can look for ways to make services more widely available. To aim to increase accessibility in a way that is also sustainable for us to continue this work in the long haul. This may be having a few sliding scale or pro-bono spots. It could mean giving back in other ways. It could be creating free or low-cost content so that more people can benefit from your knowledge and skill set. Yet even with these efforts, individual practitioners are limited in how many people they can serve at one time.

Burnout rates are already a concern for front line care providers (Lin et al, 2023; Shell et al. 2022; Zarzycha et al. 2022). Even if every single helper takes the above steps, it will still not likely be enough to meet the needs of the larger public and strained systems. A number of studies have reported overall declines in mental health in the past decade and following the COVID-19 pandemic (Garriguet, 2021; Wiens et al., 2020). In a recent Statistic Canada survey (2023) only about half of those who had met the criteria for a mood, anxiety or substance use disorder had talked to a health professional in the last year. One in three of these individuals reported unmet needs or only partially met needs for mental health services, with access to counselling or therapy reported as a higher unmet or only partially met need than information about mental health or access to medication.

This is why we also need to advocate for change on a larger system level. We need more public health funding for those who lack the financial resources to access adequate services. We need public change to advocate for support for the basic needs of living. For investment in the health and mental health of our communities, we need larger changes on social and political levels to be able to create more equitable support for all. It is a complex issue and I don't claim to have all the answers (Bongirno, 2021; Moroz et al., 2020; Statistics Canada, 2023). I hope to continue to encourage ongoing discussion advocacy and the search for creative solutions.

The Search for Safe Spiritual Support

If you are looking for support in your own journey I have put together a few options on where to start.

Ask for Referrals Within Your Network

Asking people who you already know, like and trust is a

helpful starting point. Word of mouth is a powerful tool. If many people that you trust also recommend a certain practitioner it may be worth looking into. If you know of even one person who you trust in this space ask them if they have any referral recommendations. There are already a number of spiritually open professionals out there. Many keep a low profile and often fly under the radar and are found mainly by word of mouth. Start by asking for recommendations.

Assess for Level of Possible Openness

Even if a health professional cannot guide you in the spiritual realm themselves, they still could be very helpful. Finding someone who is open can go a long way. As long as they are able to keep an open and non-judgemental mindset. If you feel safe with them and feel like you can develop trust to get what you need out of your work together. Another option is to find separate support for mental, physical, and spiritual needs. After all, no one person can meet all of our needs. It can be helpful to have more than one person who can assist with different goals and needs. Be open to finding more than one person to work with for different types of support.

Conduct an Online Search

Experiment with running an online search for different key terms in your area. Terms such as *"spiritual", "intuition/ intuitive", "holistic"* and professional title (such as: psychologist, social worker, massage therapist, etc). Check out what comes up. It may also help to expand the search outside of your area. Different professionals have different regulations around where they can see clients. You may have a whole province or state to draw from (or even around the world). With the rise of online and virtual services, this also means potential access to a larger pool of potential practitioners.

Listen to Your Gut/Intuition

Connect with your own spiritual practice and intuition in all of the recommendations above. Ask/pray for support and guidance. Ask to be guided by any teachers or professionals that can be a part of your healing. Ask to be shown who is safe to work with. Be open to signs and synchronicities. Be open to exploring any guidance you receive with openness and curiosity. I believe that our intuition can help guide us to the resources and supports that can be helpful on our path. Check-in with your intuition and gut feelings along the way. Be open to signs and synchronicities (Miller, 2021; Orloff, 1997). Remember to still proceed with discernment with any of the above paths. True trust needs to come with time and experience.

A HEARTFELT THANK-YOU TO
MY FELLOW PRACTITIONERS

If you are a professional who understands and lives in both worlds it is also my hope that this work can help to inspire you. For those who are grounded in science and also connected with the spiritual, yet quietly doing your work behind the scenes. This guidebook was also created for you. I hope this work may serve to inspire you to find ethical and professional ways to be seen in the world. Your work is needed in the world.

Spiritual work and practices are becoming more and more mainstream. The need for trusted helpers, guides and communities will continue to grow. There is a real need for approaches that integrate the various aspects of our being as spiritual and human beings. I have personally witnessed the openness that is already there in my practice. I only see this need expanding as more and more people continue to do their own healing work.

It is not about professionals taking over in spiritual spaces but learning to work within them. How we can be of service within and long side of it. Learning the roles that we can play in supporting people who need their intuition and spirituality to be honoured as a part of their healing path. I hope this work will help to spark conversations and will encourage you to find the ways that work within our own scope of practice, professional guidelines, and ethics.

CONCLUSION

Thank you for making it to the end of this guidebook. It is my sincere hope that the information we covered will be helpful and serve you well on your journey. A spiritual connection can be a very helpful and wonderful part of a full and whole life. May you find the path that best fits for you. I hope you are feeling better equipped to navigate the abundance of choices that are out there. If you are a practitioner on the path I hope this helps us all to keep growing and to remain committed to doing our own work in order to hold safer spaces for true healing and growth.

If you are looking to dive deeper into the information we have covered, I have included a reference and additional resources section at the end of this guidebook. If this work was helpful to you please join me over at: katieturnerpsycholgoy.com.

Thank you for reading and for your work in the world.

With great love and gratitude,

Katie Turner

ACKNOWLEDGMENTS

A hefty dose of gratitude to all the scientists, researchers and clinicians who have paved the way to bringing science into spirituality. Without this foundation, the work I do in the world would not be possible. Collectively you paved the way when the risks were far greater. To all the teachers and guides I have had the privilege of working with over the years. Thank you for paving the way and helping me on my own path. A huge heartfelt thank you to my clients. I have learned so much from you. You inspire me and give me hope for the future of humanity and this world. Thank you for your trust in me to be a part of this journey. To the 'fairy in the new coat'. You know who you are. You have helped to shape my work and taken me further in this space than I could have gone alone. Your courage, vulnerability and openness are an inspiration. May you fly free.

To my own family and ancestors. Thank you for giving me life and doing the best that you could with what you had and where you were at. There is so much love there. To my little one. You came to me in energetic form first. Thank you for choosing me to be your mother in this lifetime. I want to help to build a better world for you and future generations.

To my friends on this crazy journey. Thank you for keeping me grounded and helping me to know that I was not going crazy. To my accountability partner (and so much more). Thank you for your support and for holding a safe space. Thank you to my spiritual team and supports. This connection is life changing. I am grateful for this connection everyday.

With so much love and gratitude.

Katie Turner

ABOUT THE AUTHOR

Katie Turner is a Registered Psychologist, speaker and the founder of Katie Turner Psychology Inc. She holds a Master of Science Degree in Counselling Psychology from the University of Calgary. Along with several other post-graduate trainings and certifications. This is her first book but probably not her last.

Katie believes in a holistic approach to healing. She has studied a wide range of Western psychological approaches and Eastern healing techniques. Katie is passionate about helping her clients to heal the past, find more peace in the present and create their best possible future. Her mission is to bring together the science of psychology with the practice of spirituality. She offers consultation services, sessions, workshops and resources for organizations and modern-day spiritual seekers.

She lives in Calgary, Alberta Canada with her daughter and rescue dog. When she is not holding space in her practice or working on her latest project you can find her exploring the Rocky Mountains or on her yoga mat.

You can find more resources and ways to work together at: katieturnerpsychology.com

GLOSSARY OF TERMS

Ancestral Healing: the processing of exploring, discovering and healing of trauma and unresolved issues that have been passed down from previous generations within a family lineage.

Angels: a spiritual being, a protector or message from God/Universe/Spirit, present in different religious or spiritual orations. Often represented in a human form with large wings. To provide guidance, support, protection and love. Some have specific qualities and gifts.

Anti-Oppression Work: the challenging and dismantling of systems of oppression and practices. Aims to recognize the oppression that exists within society with the aim of eventually equalizing inequalities in power dynamics within a society.

Ascended Masters: an enlightened being(s) who was human in previous incarnations or lifetimes. A once ordinary human who gone through a process of spiritual initiation and transformation. Examples: Jesus, Buddha.

Breath-work: exercises or therapy that use breathing. Focus on intentionally changing breathing patterns for desired results.

Bypassing: ignoring or trying to get around something. Ignoring something you don't want to deal with. Trying to get the desired result faster. Spiritual Bypassing is the use of spiritual teachings or practices to avoid unresolved issues. Emotional bypassing is ignoring or avoiding processing unresolved emotions or feelings.

Capitalism: an economic and political system where a country's industry and trade are controlled by private individuals or businesses for profit. The system that is dominant in the Western world.

Colonialism: the policy and practice of a country taking full or partial control of another country. In most cases for the purpose of occupation and economic exploitation. An act of political and economic invasion and domination by a foreign power.

Conscious Mind: The thoughts, feelings and memories that a person is aware of having at any one given time. Believed to make up a small portion of the percentage of the mind. According to psychoanalytic theory, the mind is like an iceberg with the part above the water being conscious mind awareness.

Consciousness: awareness of what we are experiencing,

awareness of what is within us (internal) and outside of us (external) existence.

Cultural Appropriation: occurs when members of a majority group adopt the cultural elements of a minority group in a way that reinforces stereotypes, is exploitative or disrespectful.

Cultural Appreciation: the respectful borrowing of elements of another culture rooted in deeper understanding, respect and honouring of the culture of origin.

Ego: one's sense of personal self. Opinion or idea of self. Our roles and perceived sense of self. Who we believe ourselves to be in the world. Self-identity is what you perceive of as yourself.

Empath: someone who has a dominant intuitive ability of clarisentience. Someone who can feel the emotions or physical sensations of others within their own sensory experience. Someone who can take on the physical sensations (physical empathy) and/or emotions (emotional empath) of another person, people or groups.

Empirically Validated Research: any study where conclusions are only from concrete, verifiable evidence. Guided by scientific findings and evidence. Empirically validated treatments are treatments that have been scientifically studied and shown to work (more than chance).

Energy Healing: healing techniques that work with the flow of energy in the body. To balance, restore or influence the flow of energy in the body. Rooted in ancient practices such as Chinese Medicine and Ayurveda and based in the beliefs that energy flows through all living things, including our bodies. Working with the energy pathways of the body. May or may not involve physical touch.

Enlightenment: state of attaining spiritual concuss, knowledge, insights or awareness. The Buddha was believed to have achieved this state of consciousness. A state of spiritual bliss characterized by the absence of suffering or desire.

Discernment: the ability to distinguish well and to make wise decisions. To recognize what is helpful and meaningful for you and what is not. Seeing reality as it is without judgement. Being able to see and to understand what is often difficult to perceive. Spiritual understanding and awareness.

Gaslighting: psychological manipulation of someone by causing them to question their reality and or sanity, such as their memory, thoughts or logic. It can be intentional or unintentional. A form of manipulation and psychological control.

Highly Sensitive Person: 15-20% of people in a given population who have a highly sensitive nervous system. A nervous system that processes sensory information more deeply. The term is based on the research of psychosis Dr. Elaine Aron. It is a sensitive nervous system and not a psychological disorder.

Intuitive Awakening: the opening of and connection with intuitive abilities. See also: **Spiritual Awakening**.

Manifesting: The belief that our thoughts create our reality. Often used with the "Law of Attraction", that what we think about and how we feel, what we consciously focus on will create our reality and bring us what we focus on. The belief that we can "think/visualize" a goal into reality.

Meditation: techniques that help to achieve focused attention, relaxation and or a heightened state of awareness. Shown to have many positive effects on well being. There are many different types of practice and most involve an aspect of initially directing the focus on the mind.

Mediumship Abilities: the ability to communicate with someone who is deceased. Ability to communicate with the spirit world.

Patriarchy: a system of society or government where men hold the power or most of the power (at the exclusion of women and non-male genders). Traditionally where the father or oldest male is considered the head of the family and dependents are traced through the male line, property passes to the males of the family.

Past Life Healing: a process that helps individuals heal trauma from past lifetimes. Allowing for the release of negative remaining energy that impacts this lifetime. Helps to uncover and resolve trauma from past lifetimes as well as to uncover and receive gifts, knowledge and abilities from past lifetimes.

Placebo Effect: the benefit of a treatment that is due to a person's belief in the treatment (rather than the treatment itself). Research estimates that 35% of people experience a placebo effect and this can be higher in some samples.

Planifesting: The process of planning your manifestation. Combining visualizing and thinking about your goals with the planning and execution of steps to achieve them.

Restorative Justice: a system of justice that focuses on re-habilitation of offenders with reconciliation with the victims and the community at large. Allows victims of a crime and the offenders and their family/community members to come together to explore how everyone has been impacted by the offence. An approach that seeks to repair the harm done. To have those responsible for the harm to take accountability for their actions and to repair the harm caused. To address the needs of those impacted by those responsible following a crime or offence. Encourages communication and addressing the resulting harm by all those involved.

Shadow Work: practices and work that focus on the part of the psyche that are usually below conscious mind awareness. Based on the work of psychotherapist Carl Jung. Shadow work involves bringing unwanted and/ aspects of the personality into conscious awareness.

Social Justice: work focused on the fair and equitable distribution of resources, opportunity and privileges within a society.

Soul: the spiritual part of a human or animal, the part that is beloved to be immortal, immaterial or spiritual force or energy of a person or living being.

Spirit Animals: a spirit in animal forms that helps, guides or protects a person. Different animals bring different characteristics, messages and gifts to the person they are supporting.

Spirit Guides: spiritual or energy support, protection or guidance. They can bring protection, guidance, messages, and gifts. Universal forces that help us. They can show up in many different forms, including angels, animals, ancestors, mythical creatures, god(s)/goddess(es), other, etc.

Spiritual Awakening: a recognition/experience of the connection between ourselves and the world around us. An awareness or newfound awareness of spiritual reality around us. A profound shift in person of ourselves and the world around us.

Subconscious Mind: The level of mind just below the threshold of conscious awareness. With introspection you can likely notice where an impulse is coming from within this part of the mind. According to psychoanalytic theory, the mind is like an iceberg with the part below the water being the subconscious and unconscious mind awareness.

Systemic Oppression: the intentional disadvantaging of certain groups based on their identity to the advantage of other groups based on the dominant identity. Discrimination and unequal treatment of historically disadvantaged groups.

> **Racism:** oppression based on the membership of a particular race or ethnic group. Usually one that is a minority or traditionally marginalized.
>
> **Misogyny:** ingrained prejudice towards, dislike or hatred towards women.
>
> **Sexism:** discrimination based on sex. Discriminations against women.
>
> **Homophobia:** prejudice or dislike towards gay and queer people (or those who do not identify as heterosexual).
>
> **Ableism:** discrimination against those with disabilities, in favour of able bodied people.

Systemic Privilege: social and cultural advantages that are given to some people and not others, not deserved or on the basis of merit but due to identity factors.

Toxic Positivity: when a person tries to reject or suppress difficult or "negative" emotions and to only focus on more pleasant or"positive" emotions. Even when the difficult emotions are appropriate. Pressure to only express or experience positivity, optimism or gratitude, no matter how difficult the circumstances.

Toxic Spirituality: belief that difficult or negative experiences or even are bad and and should be repressed. Beliefs that promote 'love and light' and "manifesting" one's personal reality without acknowledging the impact of the human nervous system, trauma, systems of oppression or other real human challenges and struggles. Spiritual practices that promote gaslighting and victim/survivor blaming to avoid discomfort and challenging emotions.

Unconscious Mind: The level of the mind below the subconscious level of awareness. You consciously have no idea what is within the unconscious, it is not accessible with introspection or reflection alone. According to psychoanalytic theory, the mind is like an iceberg with the part below the water being the subconscious and unconscious mind awareness.

White Fragility: defensiveness and discomfort on the part of a white person in the face of information about systemic oppression, racial inequality and historic and systemic injustice. Without awareness and working through this defensiveness white fragility maintains rather than dismantles racist systems.

Aiyana, S. (2022). Becoming the one: Heal your past, transform your relationship patterns and come home to yourself. Prism.

Alberta Government (2024). Regulated health professions and colleges: Learn about the Health Professions Act (HPA) and the regulatory college that govern health professions and health professionals in Alberta. https://www.alberta.ca/regulated-health-professions

American Psychiatric Association. (2017). The diagnostic and statistical manual of mental disorders. (5th ed.) CBS Publishing.

American Psychological Association. (2017). How do I choose between medication and therapy? https://www.apa.org/ptsd-guideline/patients-and-families/medication-or-therapy

Aoun, S., Breen, L., White, I., Rumbold, B., & Kellehear, A. (2018). What sources of bereavement support are perceived helpful by bereaved people and why? Empirical evidence for the compassionate communities approach. Palliative Medicine. 32(8), 1378-1388. https://doi.org/10.1177/02692163187749

Miller, A., Isaacs, K., & Haggard, E.(1965). On the nature of the observing function of the ego. British Journal of Medical Psychology, 38(2),161-169. https://doi.org/10.1111/j.2044-8341.1965.tb00537.x

Baldessarini R., Tondo, L., Ghiani, C & Lepri, B. (2010, August 1). Illness risk following rapid versus gradual discontinuation of antidepressants. American Journal of Psychology. https://ajp.psychiatryonline.org/doi/full/10.1176/appi.ajp.2010.09060880

Bargh J., (Ed.) (2006). Social psychology and the unconscious: The automaticity of higher mental processes. Psychology Press.

Bargh, J, & Morella, E. (2008). The unconscious mind. Perspectives on Psychological Science (3)1, 73-79. https://doi.org/10.1111/j.1745-6916.2008.0006

Bhandari, S. (2023). What is Déjà vu? Retrieved on: January 16, 2024. https://www.webmd.com/mental-health/what-is-Déjà-vu.

Bongiorno, J. (2021, June 17). Canada's mental health services were already overloaded. The pandemic made it worse. Canada's National Observer. https://www.nationalob-server.com/2021/06/17/analy-sis/canadas-mental-health-services-already-overloaded-pandemic-made-it-worse

Bono, G., Emmons, R., & Mc-Cullough, M. (2004). Grati-tude in practice and the practice of gratitude. Posi-tive Psychology in Practice, 64, 464-481. https://doi.org/10.1002/9780470939338.ch29

Brown, B. (2007). I thought it was just me (but it isn't): Making the journey from "What will people think" to "I am enough". Avery.

Brown, B. (2021). Atlas of the heart: Mapping meaningful connec-tions and the language of human experience. Random House.

Cacciatore, J., Thieleman, K., Fretts, R., & Jackson, L. (2021). What is good grief support? Exploring the actors and ac-tions in social support after traumatic grief. PLOS ONE, 16(5). https://doi.org/10.1371/journal.pone.0252324

Church, D. (2009). The genie in your genes: Epigenetic medicine and the new science of intention. (2nd ed.). Cumberland House Publishing.

Clear, J. (2018). Atomic habits: An easy and proven way to build good habits and break bad ones. Avery. https://catalog.umj.ac.id/index.php?p=show_detail&id=62390

Colliner, L. (2016). Growth after trauma. Why are some people more resilient than others- and can it be taught? American Psychological Association, Monitor on Psychology. 47(10). https://www.apa.org/monitor/2016/11/growth-trauma

Corneille, J., & Luke, D. (2021).

Spontaneous spiritual awakenings: Phenomenology, altered states, individual differences, and well-being. Frontiers in Psychology, 12, 720579. https://doi.org/10.3389/fpsyg.2021.720579

Corrigan, W. & Watson, A. (2002) Understanding the impact of stigma on people with mental illness. World Psychiatry. 1(1). 16-20. https://pubmed.ncbi.nlm.nih.gov/16946807

Borges, P. & Tomlinson, K. (Directors). (2016) Crazywise. [Film] CrazyWise, LLC. Retrieved from: https://crazywise-film.com/resources/

DiAngelo, R. (2018). White fragility: Why it's so hard for white people to talk about racism. Beacon Press.

Diener, E., Ng, W., Harter, J. & Arora, R. (2010). Wealth and happiness across the world: material prosperity predicts life evaluation, whereas psychosocial prosperity predicts positive feeling. Journal of Personality and Social Psychology. 99(1). 52-61. https://doi.org/10.1037/a0018066

Dijksterhuis A, Chartrand T. & Aarts H. (2007). Automatic behavior. In: Bargh J, (Ed.). Social psychology and the unconscious: The automaticity of higher mental processes. Psychology Press. https://ci.nii.ac.jp/ncid/BA81218311

Dispenza, J. (2015). You are the placebo: Making your mind matter. Hay House Inc. http://ci.nii.ac.jp/ncid/BB19568080

Donnelly, G., Zheng, T., Haisley, E., & Norton, M. (2018). The amount and source of millionaires' wealth (moderately) predict their happiness. Personality and Social Psychology Bulletin. 44(5). https://doi.org/10.1177/0146167217744766

Ekman, P. (1972). Universals and cultural differences in facial expressions of emotion. In J. Cole (Ed.), Nebraska Symposium on Motivation, 19. 207–282. University of Nebraska Press.

Emmons, R., & Crumpler, C. (2000). Gratitude as a human strength: Appraising the evidence. Journal of Social and Clinical Psychology, 19(1), 56-69. https://doi.org/10.1521/jscp.2000.19.1.56

Epstein, S. (2010). Demystifying intuition: What it is, what it does, and how it does it. Psychological Inquiry, 21(4), 295-312. https://doi.org/10.1080/1047840x.2010.523875

McGilchrist, I. (2019). The master and his emissary: The divided brain and the making of the western word. Yale University Press.

Fang, X, Rychlowska, M. & Lange J. (2022). Cross-Cultural and inter-group research on emotion reception. Journal of Cultural Cognitive Science, 6, 1-7. https://doi.org/10.1007/s41809-022-00102-2

Frankl V. (2006). Man's search for meaning. (2nd ed.) Beacon Press.

Freud S. An autobiographical study. (1961). In: Strachey J, (Eds.) Standard edition of the complete psychological works of Sigmund Freud. Vol. 20. Hogarth Press. 7–74. Original work published 1925. http://psycnet.apa.org/record/1964-35016-000

Garriguet, D. (2021, Feb 1). Portrait of youth in Canada: Data report. Chapter 1: Health of youth in Canada. Statistic

REFERENCES

Canada. https://www150.stat-can.gc.ca/n1/en/pub/42-28-0001/2021001/article/00001-eng.pdf?st=Lc7Kufj8

Gibson, L. (2015). Adult children of emotionally immature parents: How to heal from distant, rejecting, or self-involved parents. New Harbinger Publications. https://openlibrary.org/books/OL27186268M/Adult_children_of_emotionally_imma-ture_parents

Goleman, D. (2005). Emotional intelligence: Why it can matter more than IQ. Bantam. http://ci.nii.ac.jp/ncid/BA28658620

Gottman, J. & Silver, N. (2015). The Seven Principles of Making Marriage Work. (Revised ed). Harmony. http://ci.nii.ac.jp/ncid/BB05926466

Harvard Health Publishing. (2020). Understanding the stress response. Retrieved November 22, 2021 from https://www.health.harvard.edu/staying-healthy/understanding-the-stress-response

Hassan, S. (2015). Combating cult mind control: The #1 best-selling guide to protection, rescue, and recovery from destructive cults. Freedom of Mind Press.

Hedva, B. (2013). Betrayal, trust and forgiveness: A guide to emotional healing and self-renewal. Wynword Press.

Jenkinson, S. (2015). Die wise: A manifesto for sanity and soul. North Atlantic Books.

Johnson, S. (2013). Love sense. The revolutionary new science of romantic relationships. Little, Brown Spark.

REFERENCES

Johnson, S. (2008). Hold me tight: Seven conversations for a lifetime of love.
Little, Brown Spark. https://ci.nii.ac.jp/ncid/BB1477372X

Jorm, A. (2012). Mental health literacy: Empowering the community to take action for better mental health. American Psychologist, 67(3), 231-243. https://doi.org/10.1037/a0025957

Jung, C. G. (2014). The archetypes and the collective unconscious (Collected Works of C.G Jung). (2nd ed). Routledge. https://doi.org/10.4324/9781315725642

Jung, C. (2023). Psychology of the Collective Unconscious. 7th ed. Revelation Press.

Kaheneman, D., & Deaton, A. (2010). High income improves evaluation of life but not emotional well-being. Proceedings of the National

Academy of Sciences, 107(38). 16489-16493. https://doi.org/10.1073/pnas.1011492107

Kang, L. & Pedersen, N. (2017). Quackery: A brief history of the worst ways to cure everything. Workman Publishing Company.

Kean, L. (2017). Surviving death. In Princeton University Press eBooks. https://doi.org/10.1515/9781400834600

Kendi, I. (2023). How to be an anti-racist. (2nd ed.) One World.

Killingsworth, M. (2021). Experienced well-being rises with income, even above $75,000 per year. Proceedings of the National Academy of Sciences of the United States of America, 118(4). https://doi.org/10.1073/pnas.2016976118

Klien, H, Lount, R., Park, H, & Linford, B. (2020). When goals are known: The effects of audience relative on goal commitment and performance. Journal of Applied Psychology, 105(4) 372–389.https://doi.org/10.1037/apl0000441

Kubrick, S. (2023). It's on me: Accept hard truths, discover your self, and change your life. The Dial Press.

Kyer, B. (2016). Surviving compassion fatigue: Help for those who help others. Gatekeeper Press.

Lerner, H. (2005). The dance of anger: A woman's guide to changing the patterns of intimate relationships (20th ed). Avon.

Levine, P. & Frederick, A. (1997). Waking the tiger: Healing trauma. North Atlantic Books. https://en.wiki-

pedia.org/wiki/Wak-
ing_the_Tiger

Levine, P. (2010). In an un-
spoken voice: How the
body releases trauma and re-
stores goodness. North Atlantic
Books. https://ci.nii.ac.jp/ncid/
BB06082199

Liedauer, S. (2021). Dimensions
and causes of systemic oppression. Reduced inequalities,
Encyclopedia of the UN Sustainable Development Goals. 1-11.

Lin, L., Assefa, M., & Stamm,
K. (2023, April 1). Practitioners are overworked and burned
out, and they need our support.
American Psychological Association. https://www.apa.org/
monitor/2023/04/psycholo-
gists-covid-burnout

Lindqvist, E., Östling, R., & Ce-
sarini, D. (2020) . Long-
run effects of lottery wealth
on psychological well-being.

REFERENCES

The Review of Economic Studies. 87(6). 2703-2726. https://doi.org/10.1093/restud/rdaa006

Lipton, Dr. B.(2016). The Biology of Belief. (10th ed.) Hay House Inc.

Long, J. (2014). Near-death experiences. Evidence for their reality. Missouri Medicine, 111(5), 372-380.

Lyons, M. (2019). The dark triad of personality: Narcissism, machiavellianism and psychopathy in everyday life. Academic Press.

Mental Health First Aid USA. (2020). Mental Health First Aid. Washington, DC: National Council for Mental Wellbeing.

McCarty, R. (2016). The fight-or-flight response: A cornerstone of stress research. Stress: Concepts, Cognition, Emotion, and Behavior. 33-37.

https://doi.org/10.1016/
B978-0-12-800951-2.00004-2

McCraty, R., Atkinson, M, & Bradley, R. (2004). Electrophysiological evidence of intuition: Part 1. The surprising role of the heart. Journal of Alternative and Complementary Medicine, 10(1), 133–143. https://doi.org/10.1089/107555304322849057

McCraty, R., Atkinson, M., & Bradley, R. (2004b). Electrophysiological Evidence of Intuition: Part 2. A System-Wide Process? Journal of Alternative and Complementary Medicine, 10(2), 325–336. https://doi.org/10.1089/107555304323062310

McGilchrist, I. (2019). The master and his emissary: The divided brain and the making of the western world. (2nd ed.). Yale University Press.

McGrath, T. (2019). Woke: A guide to social justice. Constable.

REFERENCES

McTaggart, L. (2008). The field: The quest for the secret force of the universe (2nd ed.). Harper Collins.

Miller ,L. (2021). The awakened brain: The new science and spirituality and our quest for an inspired life. Random House.

Mills, A., & Tucker, J. (2014). Past-life experiences. In E. Cardeña, S. Lynn. & S. Krippner (Eds.), Varieties of anomalous experience: Examining the scientific evidence. (2nd ed.). American Psychological Association. 303 –332 https://doi.org/10.1037/14258-011

Moncrieff J, Lewis, G., Fremantle, N, Johnson, S., Barnes, T., Morant, N., Pinfold, V., Hunter, R., Kent, L., Smith, R., Darton, K., Horne, R., Crellin, N., Cooper, R., Marston, L., & Priebe, S. (2019). Randomized controlled trial of gradual antipsychotic reduction and discontinuation in people with schizophrenia and related disorders: The RADAR trial (research into antipsychotic discontinuation and reduction). BMJ Open 9(11). https://doi:10.1136/bmjopen-2019-030912

Moroz, N. Moroz, I. &D'Angelo, M, (2020). Mental health services in Canada: Barriers and cost-effective solutions to increase access. Healthcare Management Forum, 33(6). https://doi.org/10.1177/0840470420933911

Moulton S. (2018). Gaslighting: Recognize manipulative and emotionally abusive people—and break free. Da Capo Lifelong Books.

Myers, D. (2000). The funds, friends, and faith of happy people. American Psychologist, 55(1), 56–67. https://doi.org/10.1037/0003-066X.55.1.56

REFERENCES

Nelson, B. (2019). The emotion code: How to release your trapped emotions for abundance, health, love and happiness. St. Martin's Essentials.

Ness, D, Heetderks Strong, K., & Derby, J. (2020). Restoring justice: An introduction to restorative justice. (6th ed). Routledge.

Nunez, K. (2020). Fight, flight, or freeze: How we respond to threats. Healthline. Retrieved November 22, 2021, from: https://www.healthline.com/health/mental-health/fight-flight-freeze#overactive-response

Orloff, J.(1997). Second sight: A psychiatrist and intuitive tells her extraordinary story...and shows you how to discover your intuitive gifts. Grand Central Publishing.

Orloff, J. (2015). The power of surrender: Let go and energize your relationships, success and well-being. Harmony.

Orloff, J. (2018). The empath's survival guide: Life strategies for sensitive people. Sounds True.

Patrick, C. (2022). Psychopathy: current knowledge and future directions. Annual Review of Clinical Psychology, 18(1), 387–415. https://doi.org/10.1146/annurev-clinpsy-072720-012851

Pescosolido, B., Halpern-Manners, A., Luo, L., & Perry, B. (2021). Trends in public stigma of mental illness in the US, 1996-2018. JAMA Network Open, 4(12), e2140202. https://doi.org/10.1001/jamanetworkopen.2021.40202

PEW Research Center (2012)The global religious landscape: a report on the size and distribution of the world's major religious groups as of

REFERENCES

2010.. Retrieved January 3, 2024 from: https://assets.pewresearch.org/wp-content/uploads/sites/11/2014/01/global-religion-full.pdf.

Prava Baral, S., Prasad, P., Raghuvamshi, G. (2022). Mental health awareness and generation gap. Indian Journal of Psychiatry, 64(3). S636 https://doi.org/10.4103%2F0019-5545.341859

Psychologists Association of Alberta (2006). A guidebook for starting and operating an independent professional practice in psychology. (2nd ed.). https://cpa.ca/cpasite/UserFiles/Documents/publications/PAA Guidebook.pdf

Rankin, L. (2022). 10 red flags signalling that your healer, therapist, spiritual teacher, psychedelic guide, or coach may be untrustworthy. https://lissarankin.com/10-red-flags-signaling-that-your-healer-

therapist-spiritual-teacher-
psychedelic-guide-or-coach-
may-be-untrustworthy/

Rankin, L. (2022). Sacred medicine: A doctor's quest to unravel
the mysteries of healing. Sounds
True.

Reddy, M (2012). Health, happiness & family constellations:
How ancestors, family systems
and hidden loyalties shape your
life, and what you can do about
it. Vervante.

Rosenberg, M. (2012). Living nonviolent communication: Practical tools to connect and
communicate skillfully in every
situation. Sounds True.

Rosmarin, D., Pargament, K.
& Koenig, H. (2020). Spirituality and mental health:
Challenges and opportuni-
ties. Psychiatry, 8(2). 92-93.
https://doi.org/10.1016/
S2215-0366(20)30048-1

Rosenberg, M. (2015). Nonviolent communication: A language of life: Life-changing tools for healthy relationships. (3rd ed). Puddledancer Press. https://antikvariat11.cz/kniha/marshall-rosenberg-nonviolent-communication-a-language-of-life-life-changing-tools-for-healthy-relationships-2003-1315792

Rothschild, B. (2022). Help for the helper: Preventing compassion fatigue and vicarious trauma in an ever-changing world: (2nd ed.). Norton Professional Books.

Saad, L. (2020). Me and white supremacy: Combat racism, change the world and become a good ancestor. Sourcebooks.

Sammons, M. & McGuinness, K. (2015, April). Combining psychotropic medications and psychotherapy generally leads to improved outcomes and therefore reduces the overall cost of are. Society for Prescribing Psychology. https://www.apadivisions.org/division-55/publications/tablet/2015/04/combininations

Sansone, R., & Sansone, L. (2010). Gratitude and well \being: the benefits of appreciation. Psychiatry, 7(11), 18.

Schoen, M. (2014). Your survival instinct is killing you: Retrain your brain to conquer fear and build resilience. Plume.

Seligman, M. E. (2002). Authentic happiness: Using the new positive psychology to realize your potential for lasting fulfillment. Free Press.

Shadbolt, C. (2022). The many faces of systemic oppression, power and privilege: The necessity of self-examination. Transactional Analysis Journal. 52(3), 259-273.

REFERENCES

https://doi.org/10.1080/ 03621537.2022.2076411

Shell, E., Hua, J., & Sullivan, P. (2022). Cultural racism and burnout among Black mental health therapists. Journal of Employment Counseling, 59, 102- 110. https://doi.org/ 10.1002/joec.12187

Singal, J. (2021). The quick fix: Why fad psychology can't cure our social ills. Farrar, Straus And Giroux.

Singer, M. (2015). The surrender experiment: My journey into life's perfection. Harmony.

Singer, M. (2007). The untethered soul: The journey beyond yourself. New Harbinger Publications.

Smith, J., & Book, S.(2008). Anxiety and substance use disorders: A review. The Psychiatric Times, 25(10), 19–23.

https://www.ncbi.nlm.nih.gov/pmc/articles/PMC2904966/

Smith L., Webster, R., & Rubin, G.(2020). A systematic review of factors associated with side-effect expectations from medical interventions. Heath Expectations, 23(4). 731-758. https://doi.org/10.1111/hex.13059

Sperber, S. (n.d.). Fight or flight response: Definition, symptoms, and examples. Berkeley Well-Being Institute. Retrieved November 23, 2021, from https://www.berkeleywellbeing.com/fight-or-flight.html

Smithsonian Institute (2022), Human Evolution research. The Smithsonian Institution's Human Origins Program. https://humanorigins.si.edu/research

Stringer, C. & Andrews, P. (2011). The complete world of human evolution (2nd ed.) Thames and Hudson.

Statistics Canada. (2023). Mental disorders and access to mental health care. Insights on Canadian society. Government of Canada. https://www150.statcan.gc.ca/n1/pub/75-006-x/2023001/article/00011-eng.htm

Stevenson, I. (1980). Twenty cases suggestive of reincarnation. University of Virginia Press.

Talbot, M (2011). The holographic universe: The revolutionary theory of reality. Harper Perennial.

Taylor, S. (2018). Spiritual science: Why science needs spirituality to make sense of the world. Watkins Publishing.

Tedeschi, R. & Calhoun, L. (1996). The posttraumatic growth inventory: Measuring the positive legacy of trauma.

Journal of Traumatic Stress. 9(3). 455-471. https://onlinelibrary.wiley.com/doi/10.1002/jts.2490090305

Tucker, J. (2021) Cases of the reincarnation type. In Kelly, E & Marshall, P. (Eds.). Consciousness unbound. Lanham, Maryland: Rowman & Littlefield.

University of Virginia (2023). Fifty years of research. https://med.virginia.edu/perceptual-studies/our-research/children-who-report-memories-of-previous-lives/fifty-years-of-research/

Van der Kolk, B. (2015). The body keeps the score: Brain, mind, and body in the healing of trauma. (2nd ed.). Penguin Books.

Viguera A., Baldessarini, R., Hegarty, J., van Kammen, D., & Tohen, M. (1997). Clinical risk following abrupt and gradual withdrawal of maintenance neu-

roleptic treatment. Archives of
General Psychiatry, 54(1), 49-55.
https://doi:10.1001/arch-
psyc.1997.01830130055011

Wegmann, J. (2021). Psychophar-
macology: Straight talk on mental health medications. (4th ed).
PESI.

Wiens, K., Bjattarai, A., Dores, A.,
Pedram, P., Williams, J., Bul-
loch, A., & Patten, S.(2019).
Mental health among Cana-
dian postsecondary students: A
mental health crisis? Canadian
Journal of Psychiatry 65(1)
30-35. https://doi.org/10.1177/
07067437198741781

Weiss, B, (1988). Many lives,
many masters: The true story
of a prominent psychiatrist, his
young patient, and the past life
therapy that changed both their
lives. Touchstone.

Weiss, B. (1997). Only love is real:

A story of soulmates reunited. Grand Central Publishing.

Weiss, B. (2005). Same soul, many bodies: Discover the healing power of future lives through progression therapy. Free Press.

Westen, D. (1999). The scientific status of unconscious processes: Is Freud really dead? Journal of the American Psychoanalytic Association, 47(4), 1061–1106. https://doi.org/10.1177/000306519904700404

Wiest, B. (2020). The mountain is you: Transforming self-sabotage into self-mastery. Thought Catalog Books.

Winfrey, O & Perry, B. (2021). What happened to you? Conversations on trauma, resilience, and healing. Flatiron Books: An Oprah Book.

Wolynn, M. (2016). It didn't start with you: How inherited family trauma shapes who we are and how to end the cycle. Penguin Life.

Woollacot, M. & Lorimer, D. Eds. (2022). Spiritual Awakening: Scientists and Academic Describe Their Experiences. Academy for the Advancement of Postmaterialist Sciences. Vol 3.

Yalom, I. (2009). Staring at the sun: Overcoming the terror of death. Jossey-Bass.

Zarzycka, B., Jankowski, T., & Krasiczyńska, B. (2022). Therapeutic relationship and professional burnout in psychotherapists: A structural equation model approach. Clinical Psychology & Psychotherapy, 29(1), 250 –259. https://doi.org/10.1002/cpp.2629

Zehr, H, Stuzman Amstutz, L., MacRae, A. & Pranis, K. (2015). The big book of restorative justice: Four classic justice & peace-

building books in one volume.
Good Books.

ADDITIONAL RESOURCES:
SUPPORTS

Crisis Supports

International Association for Suicide Prevention:

https://www.iasp.info/

https://www.iasp.info/suicidalthoughts/

Canada

9-8-8 call or text Suicide Crisis Helpline

https://www.canada.ca/en/public-health/services/mental-
health-services/mental-health-get-
help.html?utm_campaign=not-appli-
cable&utm_medium=vanity-url&utm_source=canada-
ca_mental-health

United States

National Hotline for Mental Health Crises and Suicide Prevention

https://www.nami.org/Advocacy/Policy-Priorities/Re-sponding-to-Crises/National-Hotline-for-Mental-Health-Crises-and-Suicide-Prevention

1-800-950-6264 or text HelpLine to 62640

Call or Text – 988

988lifeline.org

Spiritual Emergency Supports

Canada

Spiritual Emergency Service

Provides listening, support, information and resources for those experiencing a Spiritual Emergency.

http://spiritualemergence.net/

United States

Spiritual Emergence Network

Provides individuals experiencing psychospiritual difficulties with a specialized mental health and support service as well as information and resources.

http:// spiritualemergence.org/

American Center for the Integration of Spiritually Transformative Experiences

Provides support to individuals who have spiritually transformative experiences. Provides information, support and resources.

http://ACISTE.org

International

The International Spiritual Emergency Network

A collaboration of not-for-profit support networks around the world. Each network is run by volunteers. Support, resources and directories for those who are experiencing a Spiritual Emergency.

https://www.spiritualemergencenetwork.org/

Finding a Provider who Works with Spiritually Based Concerns

I often receive requests for recommendations for other psychologists or therapists who understand spiritual awakening and incorporate intuition into their professional practice. As registered health professionals are usually limited to the province or state where they practice I cannot provide specific recommendations for all areas. I have included general search suggestions below. I hope it can provide a helpful starting point to assist you on your journey:

Run an Online Search in Your Area

- Search terms to put into an online search engine: (In no particular order)

- Spiritually based terms such as: Transpersonal, Spiritual, Spiritual Awakening, Intuition, Holistic, Intuitive,

- AND: the professional title, such as: Psychologists, Registered Social Worker, Registered Clinical Social Workers, Psychiatrist, etc. Naturopathic Doctor, Massage therapist, Doctor of Chinese Medicine, Doctor of Chiropractic, etc.

- AND your geographical area: this may include your postal or zip code, your city, province or state.

- It may also be helpful to search for training/certifications such as those listed in the next section (providing safe and ethical support). Keep in mind that finding the right fit and someone who you are comfortable with is a more important predictor of positive change than any one technique, training or certification on its own.

Additional Directories

Psychology Today

https://www.psychologytoday.com/ca/therapists

Highly Sensitive Person Informed Therapists

https://hsperson.com/therapists/seeking-an-hsp-knowledge-able-therapist/

Therapy in Colour: The Mental Health Directory for People of Colour:

https://www.therapyincolor.org/

Open Path: Collective: Sliding Scale/Lower Cost

https://openpathcollective.org

Let people know what you want to work on and that you would prefer to be matched with someone who is open to working with the concerns and world views that are important to you. Be open about your preferences in being matched with a provider, including if spirituality is something that is important to you.

I worked in a number of nonprofits and community-based mental health organizations in my early career, and although the focus was not specialized in spiritual concerns in any of these agencies I was always eager to add those who expressed a preference for this lens in their work to my caseload when I had the chase. You might be surprised. Again, it usually doesn't hurt to ask.

If there is someone who you would like to work with but cannot afford their regular rates you can always contact them to find out if they do offer sliding scale or pro-bono slots. It doesn't hurt to ask. Even if they cannot take you on as a client they may be able to point you in the direction of someone or other resources that could be helpful.

TIPS FOR NAVIGATING THE MENTAL HEALTH SYSTEM AND FINDING THE BEST FIT

To help you answer this question of what type of mental health support might be the best fit, here is a breakdown of costs and benefits of various mental health service options that may be available to you.

(*The following is a breakdown based on this writer's experience within the mental health field within the geographical area of Calgary Alberta, Canada).

The main providers of mental health services (again, within Alberta, Canada) can generally be broken down into non-profit services, provincial health care services, School/ Academic Based Supports, Employee Assistance Programs (EAP) and Private Practice Services.

Non-Profit Community Agencies

Many services within the non-profit sector focus on clearly defined types of mental health support services. These services may range from emergency crisis counselling, walk-in mental health counselling, family counselling, sexual assault counselling, grief support or more general short terms counselling services. With the exception of certain more specialized programs the majority of non-profit supports offer services based on more of a brief support model.

The benefits of such services are that there are many skilled providers and they can be more accessible, especially if finances are a concern. For more specialized services the benefits can be connecting to a program and service tailored to your needs.

The downside can be that areas outside of the program often would require a referral. There are also areas that are more specialized and therefore agencies may not be equipped with the budget and staffing to employ specialists in certain areas. If you develop a relationship with your counsellor you may or may not be able to return to them again in the future, especially if it is a more specialized service and your concerns no longer fall within the scope of the program.

Non-profit counselling centres can also be great resources for free or low cost counselling. The downside can be long waitlist times if your concerns do not constitute an immediate safety risk. There may be less choice and control over goodness of fit with your counsellor or available appointment hours. Many centres also offer spaces for sliding scale fee arrangements for those with financial concerns. These spaces may be provided by Master's level graduate psychology or social work students, or those completing their professional registration hours or may also be offered by Registered mental health professionals. Also the majority of agencies have requirements and guidelines for determining financial needs which are often based on the poverty guidelines for Canada. They often include an assessment or proof of income and number of legal dependents. If financial concerns are based more on willingness to invest or income going to non-essential expenses rather than true financial need an individual may not qualify for reduced rates.

Health Services Supports

There are also a number of excellent services within the provincial health care system. The benefit is that in services under Provincial Health Care are most often provided at no cost to the client (regardless of income) as a part of overall health care services. There are many specialized programs and supports and like all health services patients are triaged depending on urgency and need. This can be a positive thing for those who are really struggling and are at risk.

The downside can be that for those whose needs are not as urgent may be facing varying wait list times to be connected to support.There is also the issue of confidentiality to consider. Although your records are not available to everyone there is information that may become a part of your overall health care record. This may or may not be a concern but it is important to fully understand the limitations to confidentiality and potential risks and benefits. (It is for this reason that some people may prefer to go the private route in seeking assessment and diagnosis information if this is accessible to them).

School/Academic Based Mental Health Supports

If you or your children are connected to a school or academic program, school based and academic institutions can be another resource for mental health and counselling support. The types of support and services can vary widely between school districts and specific academic programs. It would be worth inquiring about available services within your school or academic program.

The benefits for school/academic based supports are that service providers are often more familiar with the specific challenges faced by school based and academic populations. Services are often offered on site and many supports are often available at no change or included as a part of tuition fees or are available at greatly reduced costs compared to the private sector.

The downside can be a high demand for services which can result in specific eligibility requirements for services (including type of services offered, session limits and timelines for service delivery, etc.). Longer wait list times for non-urgent concerns and outside referrals may also be required for more specialized concerns.

Employee Assistance Programs (EAP)

If your employer or health benefits program is connected to an employee assistance program (EAP) provider you may have access to counselling services at no charge as a part of your overall extended health benefit plan. EAP providers are often companies that hire their own full time staff and/or contract mental health support staff and plans are purchased through employers. EAP providers can be great resources for many generalized concerns. The majority of plans focus on brief mental health support.

The downside can be that most plans also have a set number of sessions that you and/or your family may access each benefit year. Some plans will clearly communicate the session limits while others try not to directly disclose this. In most cases EAP programs do not offer specialty services so if your needs would best be met with something more long term or specialized this may not be the most appropriate option in the long run. Also if you have a connection with your counsellor and wish to return to them again in the future this may or may not be an option. It is also important to be clear on the limits of confidentially and what information is collected and shared with your employer before starting services. Most plans aim for as much confidentiality as possible but this is important to clarify as plans can range in their own specific policies and limitations.

Private Practice Providers

Private practice providers tend to be more specialized in certain niche areas (although this is not always the case). There also tends to be a lot more flexibility in terms of how your treatment is structured. If it is important to you to establish an ongoing relationship with a professional who you can reach out to when you feel the need for additional support this is one of the benefits of private practice. Private practice can be a longer term relationship and often has more flexibility. Private practice tends to work well for those who like to be able to access services in a timely fashion and have more flexibility on the types of concerns addressed and timeline for therapy while avoiding potentially more lengthy intake processes and waitlists. Also private practice providers may or may not see fewer clients overall so that they have more energy to give to each client. There may be more options for appointment times, such as evenings and weekends. They may offer a higher standard for service provision in terms of office location, decor and overall ambience. The client often has more control and flexibility in selecting the right therapist to work with, which may increase the likelihood of a good fit. Goodness of fit between client and therapist is the number one predictor of positive change within therapy.

Depending on the nature of your concerns over time there

still may be times where your private practice therapist may (and should) refer you to another professional when concerns fall outside of their areas of expertise or if there may be a conflict of interest, one therapist may not be able to meet all your needs over time.

The downside to private practice may be the cost of services. Therapy within private practice may require a significant investment of time and resources. Depending on your health benefit provider many people do receive a yearly amount of coverage for mental health services provided by a Registered Psychologist or Registered Social Worker. This may or may not be enough to cover your treatment depending on the frequency and severity of concerns. If finances are an area of concern and it would put you in a stressful situation to invest in private services it may be a better option to go with a non-profit, provincial health service, an EAP provider, or combination of supports.

For anyone who is looking for support and what might be helpful please keep in mind that it is important to find the right fit in terms of who you work with first and foremost. There is no one technique that works for everyone and it can take time to find the right practitioners and approaches that fit for you.

If you feel this information would be helpful for anyone you care about please pass this information along. This breakdown is available for free to anyone who could benefit over at: https://katieturnerpsychology.com/blog/tips-for-navigating-the-mental-health-system-and-finding-the-best-fit

I hope this helps you to find the right fit for your needs.

ADDITIONAL RESOURCES: PROVIDING SAFE & ETHICAL SUPPORT

I often receive requests for advice on how to incorporate spirituality into a professional practice. As each professional and regulatory body has their own professional standard and guidelines I cannot speak to every situation. I have included key factors to consider and possible resources for more information and training to assist you on your search. If you are a professional provider who is interested in incorporating spiritually based work into your practice this section is for you.

First and foremost always keep up to date with and check the ethical guidelines and standards of your own profession. Know the requirement and any possible limits to your own licensing and registration.

For anyone who is new to their own spiritual awakening I would not recommend working with others, especially in a professional capacity until you are strongly grounded and clear in navigating your own intuition. Just like any new training there are multiple parts to the process before holding space for clients. First there is the necessary training and grounding in the skills and theories along with supervision and consolation and practice hours. Training in developing your own intuition may come in professional or more alternative contexts.

Look for approved trainings and evidenced based models that work well with the integration of intuition. In order to work with the public most registered health professionals are required to use evidence based models and theories.

Under this framework here are some of the trainings and certifications that can be a helpful path for mental health providers. Be sure to check what would be a good fit for your registration needs.

The following section is not meant to be an exhaustive list and is not a direct recommendation for any program. Use your own best judgement and do your due diligence in your own research.

Energy Psychology Trainings

The Association for Comprehensive Energy Psychology (ACEP)

http://www.energypsych.org

EFT Universe

https://eftuniverse.com/certification/clinical-eft-certification/

Eden Energy Medicine

https://edenenergymedicine.com/#

The Gary Craig Official EFT Training Centres

https://www.emofree.com/

Family Constellations

Hellinger Institute

https://www.hellingerinstitute.com/family-constellations-trainings/

Hakomi Training

Hakomi Institute

https://hakomiinstitute.com/workshopstrainings/up-coming-workshops-trainings

Hypnosis

Alberta Clinical Hypnosis Society

https://www.clinicalhypnosis.ca/training

Indigenous Focusing-Oriented Therapy

Focusing Initiatives International

https://focusinginternational.org/about/aboriginal-focusing-oriented-therapy-initiative/

Internal Family Systems

Internal Family Systems Institute

https://ifs-institute.com/

Jungian and Post-Jungian Therapeutic Practice

International Association for Jungian Studies

https://jungstudies.net/

Mindfulness Training for Professionals

https://positivepsychology.com/mindfulness-training-courses-programs-workshops-degrees/

Past Life Regression Therapy

Dr. Brian Weiss

https://www.brianweiss.com/5-day-training-workshops/

Psychedelic Assisted Therapy

https://www.atmajourney.com/

Transpersonal Psychology

Association for Transpersonal Psychology

http://www.atpweb.org/

Trauma Processing Therapies

Eye Movement Desensitization and Reprocessing (EMDR)

EMDR Center of Canada

https://emdrcenterofcanada.com/training/

EMDR International

https://www.emdria.org/emdr-training/

Progressive Counting

https://www.ticti.org/training/progressive-counting/

Accelerated Resolution Therapy

https://acceleratedresolutiontherapy.com/types-of-training-available/

Brainspotting

https://brainspotting.com/trainings/

Somatic Experiencing International

https://traumahealing.org/training/

Deep Brain Reorienting

https://deepbrainreorienting.com/training/

Universities & Education Centres

Sofia University

https://www.sofia.edu/

Pacifica Graduate Institute

https://www.pacifica.edu/

Omega Institute

https://www.eomega.org/

I hope this helps spark curiosity and potential to bring spirituality into your life and professional practice in ethical and evidence-based ways. I wish you all the best in your personal and professional path.